SCOTCH IN MINIATURE

A Collector's Guide
by
Alan Keegan

New and revised edition

Illustrations by Mairi Hedderwick

Northern Books from Famedram

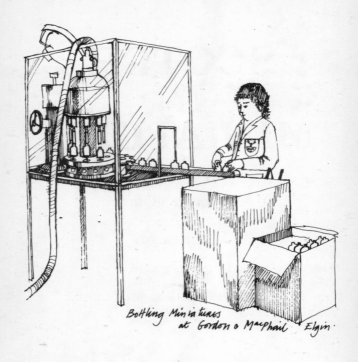

Bottling Miniatures
at Gordon o MacPhail Elgin.

Made in Scotland.
ISBN 0 905489 45 4
First published 1982. Reprinted and revised 1983, 1984, 1986 and 1988.
New edition © Copyright 1991 Famedram Publishers and Alan Keegan.
Printed and Published in Scotland for Northern Books
by Famedram Publishers Ltd. Mill Business Centre AB41
Ellon Aberdeenshire.

Contents

Introduction

Since the original publication of this book, many changes have taken place in the small world of whisky miniatures. There has been a notable increase in the number of single malts available in the 5cl format: this is good news for the collector and is most welcome to the connoisseur, whose tasting experience may thereby be widened without commitment to the purchase of a full 75cl bottle.

There has been significantly greater use of miniature whiskies for promotional use, especially by hotels and stores. There has also been wider use of 5cl bottles to mark special occasions, both public and private. Since from their nature, these bottlings are likely to be available for a limited time or only within a small area, they will form a prized part of any collection.

Travellers abroad will have noted some handsome miniatures issued for the promotion of Scotch Whisky brands outside Britain. On the home market, too, there has been some welcome improvement in presentation: more use is now made of cartons and tubes and there are more 'true' replicas of standard bottlings, especially among the malts.

Another, less welcome, development is the proliferation of miniature labels issued for their own sake. While the uninitiated collector may confuse these for real 'brands', it is hoped that most collectors will learn to recognise labels that are printed only for his attention and will find wide enough scope for his hobby among whiskies issued for good reason (as samples, as commemorative souvenirs or as promotional material).

The second part of this book, dealing with malt whiskies, is addressed particularly to those enthusiasts who use miniatures as tasting samples. Hopefully, the information will help the keen collector to a greater enjoyment of a fascinating hobby.

January 1991

Acknowledgements

In writing this book, I have been helped by many friends in the whisky trade. In particular, David Urquhart of Gordon and MacPhail has been of great assistance when compiling the lists. It has been possible to check the stocks of only a selected number of retailers, so that readers may find that other miniatures are available locally.

I am grateful to Jack Richmond of Newtonmore, who has cheerfully permitted me to plunder his great store of knowledge of all aspects of Scotch Whisky.

My wife has suffered long while I struggled with fact and syntax. To her and to the spouses of all committed whisky people, whether bottle collectors or imbibers, this book is dedicated.

When revising the lists of malt whisky miniatures I have been assisted by a number of collectors. I would like particularly to thank Mike Barbakoff, Derek Taylor and Alex Barclay for their help.

· Caol Ila ·

Some History

The first written record of a spirit distilled in Scotland from malted barley was in 1494 but the earlier story of *usquebaugh* is unknown. It seems likely that knowledge of distilling came to Scotland from Ireland some centuries before that first record.

The first 'named' whisky was Ferintosh, from the village in Ross-shire where Duncan Forbes of Culloden earned government protection for a distilling operation in the late seventeenth century.

During the eighteenth century high taxation encouraged illicit distilling, particularly in the remoter districts of the counties of Banff and Inverness. The modern era of the whisky industries dates from 1823 when the Whisky Act made legal distilling more profitable than smuggling. Shortly afterwards a practical continuous still was patented, leading to the growth of the big Lowland grain distilleries. Later in the nineteenth century the absence from the English market of brandy through decimation of the French vineyards opened the way for the expansion of whisky sales.

In the middle years of the nineteenth century, grain and malt distillers sold their products independently. The idea of mixing different whiskies was first applied to malts, eg in Usher's 'Old Vatted Glenlivet'; from this, it was only a short step to mixing the cheap (but bland) grain whiskies with the more expensive flavourful malts. Soon, the great whisky barons, Haig, Buchanan, Dewar and Mackie, who were entrepreneurs of blended whiskies rather than distillers, took over the destinies of the Scotch whisky trade.

Casks, sometimes of capacity as little as five gallons, were the first containers of whisky. Merchants

sold to dram shops and inns in large stoneware jars which were often protected by an outer basket of wicker. The dram shops catered for the 'carry out' trade by filling customer's own flagons or jugs. It was only late in the nineteenth century, where the big blending houses developed their own brand names, that the bottling of whisky became common.

Even in the earliest days of the trade it is likely that small bottles were filled as samples. There is a record of the finding of a labelled medicine type bottle of Glen Grant under the floor of the town hall in Rothes, apparently left there by the builders in 1900. The issuing of miniature bottles as we know them developed in the United States. Triffon (see p57) lists a miniature Bourbon Whiskey name Fulton dating from about 1910.

The first miniatures of Scotch Whisky seem also to have been issued for the American market, as part of the great promotional drive that followed upon the repeal of prohibition in 1933.

The earliest miniatures were corked and sealed in various ways. The Black and White miniature from this time was accompanied by a wire corkscrew to facilitate access to the contents.

Collecting Miniature Whiskies

An interest in miniature Scotch whiskies often comes from a desire to collect and display them, rather than from the expectation of enjoying their contents. The collector, faced with a long list of available miniatures, may be discouraged if his budget is small and space for display is limited. Fortunately, there is scope for specialising, so that a collection of as few as a dozen miniatures can have real significance, if buying has been purposeful.

If the collector decides to concentrate on malt whiskies, he might start with a representative from each of the tasting areas *(see p43)*. The collection may then be built up, as quickly as funds and space allow, like this:

1. One example from each tasting area. Target 9
2. Specialise in a particular area : eg Speyside. Target 30
3. A miniature from each distillery. Target 104
4. A miniature for each strength and age. Target 220
5. Every variation in label and bottle. Target 300+

Because of the now sometimes bewildering profusion of labels, blended whiskies are not so easily divided into categories. However, some degree of specialisation is possible:

6. Collect 'true' miniatures only *(see page 12)*
7. Seek out the de luxe blends
8. Restrict collecting to miniatures, whatever their shape, of those whiskies that are marketed in standard bottles.
9. Specialise in miniatures issued for promotion of products other than whisky. *(see page 22)*
10. Seek out commemorative miniatures. *(see page 24)*

Other possibilities for specialisation may be suggested by the topics covered in the pages that follow.

OBAN   BLACK & WHITE   DEWARS DE LUXE   ARGYLL   THE BALVENIE   BALVENIE PURE MALT   THE ANTIQUARY   DIMPLE   WHITE HEATHER   THE GLENLIVET   HOUSE OF COMMONS

Enjoying Miniature Whiskies

The collector who is also a whisky drinker, particularly one who is fond of malts, has an easier basis for specialising; he can restrict his collecting to miniatures of the whiskies he has sampled. He is less likely to share the view of many collectors who are reluctant to display empty miniatures.

Specialisation involves research and this will help to give point to what otherwise might be a sterile process of mere acquisition. It is the recurrent theme of this book that whether miniatures are bought as samples for tasting or as collector's pieces, the enjoyment of the process will be the greater if the purchaser is interested in the special character of the whisky as well as in the container and the label.

Definitions

MALT WHISKY is produced in pot stills, using malted barley as the base material. The process is intermittent, one batch being completed before the next is put in the still. Modern distilleries may be highly mechanised but they follow closely on 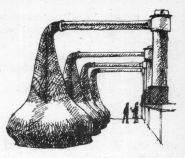 traditional methods, so that each distillery produces a whisky of uniquely distinctive character. When bottled on its own, the product of a distillery is a **single malt**.

VATTED MALTS are blendings of the products of two or more malt distilleries. Bottlers do not use the word 'vatted' on their labels, preferring the less specific terms 'pure malt' or '100% malt'.

GRAIN WHISKY is produced by a continuous process in patent stills. A fermented 'wash' of grain (usually maize, but with some malted barley) is fed into the still and the alcohol is collected at the end of the process. The patent still operates at a higher temperature than the pot still and is more efficient but much flavour is lost, so that the whiskies from the different grain distilleries have little distinctive individuality. The products of both malt and grain distilleries must be matured for three years before the spirit may legally be termed whisky.

BLENDED WHISKY contains both malt and grain whiskies. The proportion of each depends on the requirements of the bottler regarding cost and quality. Standard blends usually contain about 30% malt whiskies; a de luxe blend will probably have a higher proportion of malt but a cheap brand will certainly have much more grain.

True Miniatures

In this book, a 'true' miniature is one which fairly reproduces on a small scale the appearance of a standard (75cl) bottle. There is a special satisfaction to be had from possessing these replicas, particularly if the shape of the larger bottle or the design of its label is pleasing or unusual.

The production of a bottle of non-standard shape is expensive. In the field of miniatures, such expense is likely to be incurred only if the bottling is to be very large or very prestigious. Fortunately, the bottling of malt whiskies is quite frequently considered to fall into the latter category. Tormore, Knockando, Cardhu, Dalwhinnie, Highland Park and Isle of Jura are fine examples of special shapes replicated in miniature style.

It is possible that the improvement in presentation of miniature whiskies in recent years may owe something to the excellent example of the Japanese whisky industry.

Among blended whiskies, the tendency for 'true' miniatures to be withdrawn in favour of the 'airline' format, noted in earlier editions, has been eased if not reversed. However, the introduction of handsome miniatures like Dunhill 'Old Master' and Whyte & Mackay's 21 year old does not quite make up for the loss of many older special shapes. Of course, standard shaped miniatures can be very attractive. Subtle changes in design may enhance the appearance of the labels while remaining essentially true to the 75cl version.

Miniature Bottles, Red Lead and Painting on a Small Scale

It is an interesting and surprising fact that, in its original meaning, the word 'miniature' had nothing at all to do with smallness. The present usage is influenced by the similarity in sound to the Latin word for smaller (minor) and smallest (minimus).

The word 'miniature' comes from the Italian *miniate*, meaning to paint with minium or red lead. This substance was used as a base for the intricate work of illuminating manuscripts. The term 'miniatura' was subsequently applied to intricately painted small portraits and to any painting done on a small scale. It was an easy step from this usage to the present dictionary definition of 'miniature' as "a small or reduced copy of anything".

Oddly enough, when they refer to miniatures in Italy, they speak not of 'miniatura' but of 'mignon' or 'mignonette', from the French!

Proof

Whisky contains water as well as alcohol. When we speak of 'proof', we are concerned with the relative amount of water in the whisky.

In an early test of proof, alcohol was mixed with gunpowder and a match applied: the alcohol was under proof if the mixture failed to ignite, over proof if it exploded and 'proof' if it burned with a steady blue flame. When strength came to be measured more scientifically with a hydrometer, the amount over or under proof was measured in degrees, 'proof' being 100° in the old British 'Sikes' system.

Since 1980, when Britain subscribed to the International Organisation of Legal Metrology, we have adopted the continental (Gay Lusac) system, in which the alcohol content is expressed as a percentage of the total volume of the spirit at 20°. Under the Sikes system, standard bottling of whisky was at 70° proof. The equivalent today is 40°GL or 40% vol. In terms of the measurement used in America, this is 80° proof (US).

Malt whisky is normally distilled at between 115° and 120°. It is slightly reduced in strength before being placed in casks for maturation at about 110° (63% vol.). Since alcohol evaporates more quickly than water, the maturing whisky gradually loses strength, but is it normally necessary to add water before bottling.

It is possible to buy some malts at the strength they come from the maturing cask. 'As We Get It' labelling of Balvenie and Macallan were early examples. Some 'Signatory Vintage', some later Cadenhead and all MacArthur malts are bottled at cask strength.

IOLM/GL (%)	Sikes °Proof	American °Proof	
40	70	80	Standard strength, UK market
43	75	86	Export strength. Standard US
46	80	92	
57	100	114	'Proof'
65.5	114.6	131	Craigellachie, MacArthur bottling
100	173.35	200	Pure (absolute) Alcohol

Disappearing Miniatures

All the miniature bottlings of blended whiskies listed were available at the time of writing, though some can be purchased only in a few specialist shops.

However, supplies can be fickle and some may soon vanish from the shops. Many once-familiar miniatures like Crawford's Five Star, grace only the shelves of the longer established collectors. Other blended whiskies which were listed in the first (1982) edition and which are now quite unobtainable, include: Benmore, Glayva, Glenfoyle, Jamie Stewart, Macgregor's, Mcleay Duff, Red Hackle, Something Special (a fine decanter shape) and Usher's Old Vatted.

Occasionally there are surprise reappearances. Dimple Haig, for example, had been off the market for a number of years when the familiar 'pinch' miniature was re-introduced to celebrate the launch of Dimple as a 12 year old whisky.

The dumpy square shape of Dewar's Ancestor has also made a come-back in some UK shops, after many years as an 'export only' brand.

Discarded malt whisky labellings, some of which may have been available only a short time and in small quantities, are unlikely ever to be resurrected. The eight year old Dalwhinnie and the first label of the same malt at 15 years old, are good examples of how fleeting such issues can be. Very few of the malt whisky miniatures which were noted as currently obtainable in the first edition, can now be acquired except as 'swaps' from other collectors.

Label, Language and the Quality of Blends

The description on the label of a miniature blended whisky may not be a reliable guide to the contents. Details of strength and capacity often go unrecorded. There may even be a better known parent company behind the name of the bottler.

Some whisky companies show a remarkable want of modesty when describing their product. The most ordinary blend is 'special', 'choice' or 'the finest'. A product declared on the label to be 'old', 'rare' or even both old and rare, may be quite young for a whisky. We come to accept these terms as embroidery.

The description 'de luxe' is more reliable, this being applied by whisky companies to their premium (as distinct from their standard) blends. A similar use is made of the word 'reserve'.

Some blends carry an indication of age on the label. When this occurs, every constituent whisky in the blend, grain as well as malt, must by law have attained that age at the time of bottling. Although many premium blends declare themselves to be twelve years old, abscence of a stated age does not mean that the blend lacks mature malts or that the whisky is inferior to a 12 year old. Other factors that determine the character of a blend are the proportion of malt whisky to grain and the quality of the constituent malts.

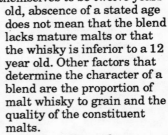

The products of some distilleries are more prized by blenders. The use of such 'crack' malts as Cragganmore, Glenlivet and Macallan, affects the cost of the blend and, in the final analysis, it will be the taste of the whisky and not the words on the label that will determine how well a whisky is appreciated.

Variants

The lists of blended miniatures include only one entry for each brand and only major and recent variations are recorded in the notes. Many collectors will be content to have just one miniature for each brand. Other will want to acquire major variants while the fanatical few will consider even the smallest change in label or bottle format a good reason for adding another miniature to their collection. It is not practical to attempt to list all variants but some of the things to look for are suggested in the following notes. Collectors who are keen to find out about all variants are advised to contact the Mini Bottle Club whose members regularly exchange information on this matter and similar subjects *(see page 57)*.

BOTTLE SHAPES: Proprietory blends may be issued with the same label in a variety of formats, according to their intended use. Black and White, for example, has been issued as a tall round, a flask and a flat 'airline' miniature.

Miniatures issued by Douglas Laing & Co are filled in several different bottles, according to the wishes of the particular customer.

Sometimes a standard shaped bottle has been used when a fancy shape has been temporarily unavailable. Examples are Aberlour 9 year old, Cardhu and Tormore 10 year old.

DIFFERENT CAPS: Most such variants are probably casual. Tartanpak flasks can have gold, red or white caps. Some miniatures may appear either with or without the name printed on the cap.

REDESIGNED LABELS: Like many other products, whiskies may receive new labels to reflect new notions of design quality. Some changes are more radical than others and probably herald a marketing campaign.

STRENGTH AND CAPACITY: There were many instances of variations following the introduction of metric measurements. Local regulations lead to much variety in detail on labels used on exported miniatures. At one count, Dewars had 63 differently worded labels for their 'White Label' miniatures.

Shapely Bottles, Pretty Labels

A shapely bottle and a colourful. well-designed label may influence the purchase of a miniature as much as the name of the whisky. That a miniature is pleasing to look at is a good reason for choosing to buy it, if the contents are not likely to be consumed. However, if the small bottle contains malt whisky and is intended for sampling, its appearance may not matter greatly.

The labels on many miniatures are scaled-down versions of those on the 75cl bottle and this is good if both containers have the same general shape. But if, for example, the miniature is a flask while the label was designed for a standard round bottle, the combination can be unattractive. Compare the appearance of the tall round miniatures issued by Gordon & MacPhail to the Tartanpak flasks with the same label. Exact scaling down of the 75cl label may result in some details being almost unreadable; it takes a keen eye to decipher the small print on the labels of Signatory Vintage miniatures.

Recent trends have been towards pictorial labels. Notable examples among malt miniatures are the labels issued by United Distillers for the malts previously marketed by Bell's. On the other hand, labels using simple lettering only can be most pleasing: Macallan and Laphraoig are two that resist the trend towards colour with conspicuous success.

One of the prettiest labels is on Cadenhead's Putachieside. Sadly, the original printing plates were lost and the re-issued label does not have the same quality as the older one.

Thistle blend, Tobermory malt and Stag's Breath liqueur have labels directly printed onto the bottle. Highland Park twelve year old has a transparent label stuck on, to give the same appearance as the directly printed one on the 75cl bottle.

Miniatures and Literature

Scottish literature abounds in references to whisky, but it would seem that our writers have not been interested in their national drink in small containers, so that we have to turn to an English author for a literary reference to whisky miniatures. Readers of Graham Green's *Our Man in Havana* will recall Wormold's memorable game of draughts with the captain of police. Miniatures were used for counters and the winner of each piece drank the contents. It was Scotch vs Bourbon and it was Scotch that, by losing the game, won the tactical battle.

The book was written in the late fifties and collectors may be interested in the whisky miniatures named: Cairngorm ("An unfamiliar whisky ... it found a raw spot on Wormold's tongue"). Dimple, Red Label, Dunosdale Cream and Old Argyll are no longer on the market. George IV and Red Label are now export only. Only the 'unfamiliar' Cairngorm eludes identification.

Whisky miniatures themselves have little to offer by way of literary references. There is 'Robbie Burns' and 'Immortal Memory' and a slightly embellished quotation from Tam o'Shanter on the label of Uisge Beatha:

> "Wi' tipenny ale, we fear nae evil;
> Wi' usqubae, we'll face the devil."

'Own Label' Miniature Whiskies

The practice by which merchants and others have their own label placed on somebody else's product has become widespread in the field of miniature whiskies. From their nature, these bottlings should usually be obtainable only from the proprietor of the label. Some of the miniatures that fall into this category contain 'own brand' whiskies, specially blended and bottled for the proprietors. At the other end of the scale there are instances where enterprising collectors have re-labelled a few standard miniatures to create a reserve of exclusive 'swaps'. Between these extremes, it is not always easy to judge the legitimacy of the labelling. In general, the ordinary collector will probably be guided by the quality of the presentation; this should lead him to reject many of the re-labelled items, as they are too often dull and unimaginative.

Some of the 'own label' miniatures that are most likely to be found are mentioned below:

STORES

Harrods have their own bottlings of both blended and malt whiskies and they have 'true' miniatures on sale exclusively in the Knightsbridge store. The Scotch House has its own miniature, while Marks and Spencers periodically issue 5cl bottles in their presentation packs. Baxter's of Speyside have small flasks of a blend and a malt whisky on sale at their Fochabers factory with the label 'Mr George Baxter's Cellar'.

A considerable number of small licensed shops in the north and west of Scotland have their own labels, many placed on the miniatures at a single source!

In the early eighties, Lambert Brothers bottled miniatures for a number of stores in the USA. The labels are uniform in style and rather dull; some of these miniatures, which include such names as 'Murnanes', 'Leland's' and 'Rochambeau' may still be bought at specialist retailers.

HOTELS

Craw's Nest, Turnberry and Post House are three hotels that have had miniatures with distinctive labels. Inverlochy Castle Hotel had an interesting miniature, now a collector's piece, of its 'Grand Reserve Whisky'.

Craw's Nest

SCOTCH WHISKY

Less distinguished are the many labels printed uniformly white on green bottles, for smaller hotels and restaurants throughout Scotland, by a Kilmarnock firm.

STATELY HOMES

Glamis Castle, Hopetoun House and Cawdor Castle have all had their own miniatures. The first two marked the final appearance of the old Stewarts of Dundee 'Watch Glass' flasks. Cawdor has a blend (Thane of Cawdor) and a Speyside malt. 'Argyll' whisky is specially associated with Inveraray Castle. Some miniatures have connections with Scottish estates: Glenmoriston Old Farm has both a blend and a vatted malt, while Dalchully had a special labelling of 15 year old Speyside malt.

The House of Commons blend, bottled by Buchanans, is one of the most handsome 'own label' miniatures; it is available only at the Palace of Westminster.

Dalchully

21

Miniatures Used for Promotion of Products Other than Whisky

Whisky miniatures which are used purely for product promotion are not likely to be found in retail shops. They will be given away at exhibitions or trade fairs and the collector will need some luck to come across them. However, possession of such exclusive miniatures will help lend interest to a collection. A few examples:

Cashmere Blend – The original issue by a firm of high-class yarn manufacturers was part of a larger package promoting a new venture into the making of knitwear. There have been two different labels and the miniature on its own is sold at the company's Elgin showroom.

Scotland's For Me – This is a case of Scotland promoting itself through its own most famous product. The Scottish Tourist Board issued the label as part of its 'Scotland's For Me!' campaign. The original flat bottling by Whyte & Mackay was never available for purchase but a later version, using Highland Queen miniatures, was sold through specialist shops.

British Rail – Several miniatures were used to promote different aspects of British Rail's service, including 'Highspeed Dram', 'Sweet Dreams' and 'Speedlink Dram'. Most unusual was the miniature designed to promote the Advanced Passenger Train. With the slogan 'The Fastest Dram on the West', the label was in the shape of the engine of the train and being on a triangular Grant's bottle, was intended to be displayed on its side.

Love of Scotland – Originally given away to customers at a trade fair, this miniature which promotes the services of a wholesaler of books, can now be found in specialist shops. A miniature issued to celebrate the first edition of the present book was never put on sale to the general public.

Surely one of the most attractive – and perhaps the most prestigious – special labellings must be that issued on a Macallan miniature to publicise the business of a finance company, ICFC.

Miniature Whiskies as Souvenirs

Any Scotch whisky miniature is a fitting 'minding' of a visit to Scotland and many thousands of standard blends and malts are purchased for this purpose each year. Until the mid '80s, surprisingly little attempt was made to exploit Scotland's national drink as a souvenir, by issuing appropriate labels. However, there has recently been a proliferation of special labels for particular places and attractions. Not all of these have been well designed and for most of them the whisky contents is incidental: Many fall within the scope of the chapter on 'label printing' *(see page 25)*.

Gordon and MacPhail pioneered the packaging of malt whisky miniatures with their 'Tartanpaks'. Many others are now marketed in presentation boxes or drums and make excellent gifts. Some standard blended miniatures have names or labels that are specially appropriate as souvenirs. Some examples are: Grouse, Beneagles, Isle of Skye, Spey Cast, Ben Alder, Hielanman, Thistle, White Heather and Glasgow's Whisky of 1990.

Little use has been made of the tartan in whisky labelling. Clan Blend, Hielanman, Inver House and Real Mackenzie are examples from the blends. The garb of the two highlanders on the Glen Grant miniature is the only example among the current malt whisky labels.

There are a few instances of Gaelic being used on miniature labels. 'Te Bheag' is 'The little woman' and 'Poit Dhubh' is 'Black Pot', the Highlander's name for, respectively, his dram and an illicit still. 'Uisge Beatha' might seem an appropriate enough name for a Scotch whisky, though it is ironic that when this Gaelic expression, meaning 'Water of Life', passed into the English language, it was the first part, meaning water, that was adapted to 'whisky'.

Whisky Miniatures for Special Occasions

Royal events had been commemorated on flagons, but the wedding of the Prince of Wales seems to have been the first to be marked by special miniature bottlings. The most popular was in flat 'airline' format with a portrait label. The three malts issued on the same occasion by Gordon & MacPhail were unusual, in that they were vattings of whiskies distilled in 1948 and 1961, the respective birth years of Prince Charles and Lady Diana Spencer. Many subsequent royal occasions have been marked by the issue of miniature bottles or flagons.

Among the malts, Glenfarclas has been used to celebrate the 750th anniversary of the city of Berlin and the 25th year of the Elgin Round Table.

Clynelish helped mark Embo's 'day of freedom' in the summer of 1989, with a special labelling.

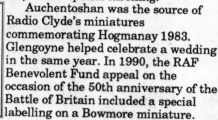

Auchentoshan was the source of Radio Clyde's miniatures commemorating Hogmanay 1983. Glengoyne helped celebrate a wedding in the same year. In 1990, the RAF Benevolent Fund appeal on the occasion of the 50th anniversary of the Battle of Britain included a special labelling on a Bowmore miniature.

Miniatures in very limited numbers have been issued to mark successive meetings of the Siberian Husky Club at Aviemore. There have been 'wee bottles' to celebrate the centenary of Celtic FC and of the building of the Forth rail bridge. The Garden Festivals at Liverpool, Glasgow and Gateshead have seen the issue of miniatures.

Miniatures have been presented to delegates at some licensed trade events. Whyte & Mackay marked the 1981 conference of the Scottish Licensed Trade Association – and the royal wedding of that year – with a special label. In the two following years delegates also received souvenirs. The SLTA conference of 1986 was chaired by Bell's and those attending were presented with small white bells bearing an appropriate message.

Label Printing

A stamp collector who takes his hobby seriously will be quick to recognise a stamp that has been issued just for the collector. Having recognised its purpose he will probably reject it, preferring to collect only those stamps that are genuinely issued for postal reasons.

Collectors of miniature whiskies are now faced with a similar situation, with new labels (rather than new whiskies, suitably labelled) being issued only because there are collectors who will buy them.

Because of the economics of printing, labels tend to come in batches. Sometimes there is an obvious connecting theme: In Mr Lambert's 'Munro' series, each label records the name and height of a Scottish mountain over 3000', with a possible limit of 279. The 'Mist' miniatures bear the reproduction of a painting relevant to each location. The 'Campbeltown Commemorative' series catalogues the names and dates of the 24 distilleries that have existed in that town.

Another class of label now appearing on whisky miniatures involves concocted 'brand' names. Many of these incorporate Scots idioms and tourist themes; a good number of them are designed to amuse.

The firms who issue these labels simply respond to an obvious demand from inveterate collectors. Collectors who have not yet entered this category and whose hobby is based on a genuine interest in whisky, must be selective in their purchasing. There are sufficient miniature whiskies issued for promotional reasons, as commemorative souvenirs or as samples, to satisfy the collecting urge in most of us.

If one of these labels is acquired, there is compensation for the collector who does not want to display it. He can realise its value by drinking the whisky; there is no consolation like this for the philatelist who acquires a dud stamp!

Jugs, Jars, Flagons, Flasks

In the thirties and early post-war years, a popular souvenir of a visit to Scotland was a miniature stoneware flagon, often filled with an un-named Scotch whisky and carrying an appropriate message. 'Cheers from Tomintoul' and 'A Wee Deoch an Doras from Braemar' are examples of the genre. Such jars are no longer found, except in antique shops, though a similar stoneware miniature has been available at the Glendronach distillery shop. A miniature of the stylish Glenfiddich 'crock' has been sold without content at the distillery.

Miniature flagons are still produced and though they are often thought of as novelties rather than small containers, they do have historic relevance, being replicas of the kind of domestic vessel used before bottled whisky became the norm. The Usquaebach miniature is unusual: It is a copy of an old two or three gallon storage jar, rather than the usual pint flagon. The container was made specially for a store in America but has been sold in this country.

One of the most familiar flagons in the export market is that containing 'Ye Whisky of Ye Monks'; it is produced in both 75cl and 5cl sizes; the latter may sometimes be found in shops in the UK.

Miniature Flagons

There follows a list of the miniature whisky flagons that may be found in shops, particularly at tourist centres in Scotland.

MARKETED BY DOUGLAS LAING & CO

Bar Scotch		
Clydebank		
DL13		
Eaton's		
House of Peers	White/	
Kentshire	Green/	Paper seal
King of Scots	Black	
Langside		
McGibbons		
Raleigh		
Scotch Select		
Whiteinch		
King of Scots 17	White, Red Lion	Hexagonal
King of Scots 25	Maroon	Spode Decanter
Old Glasgow	Black	Paper seal
Usquaebach	Cream/tan	Paper seal

MADE BY RUTHERFORDS

Game Birds	White	4 different decorations
Castles	with tops in	3 different pictures
Hunting Scenes	several	5 different scenes
Ships	colours	6 different pictures

OTHERS

Bowmore 10yo	white	Gateshead Garden Festival
Chequers	green	boxed
Columba Cream	tan	whisky liqueur
Glen Fiona	cream/green top	various/wax seal
Royal Salute	blue/green/brown	
Souvenir	black	paper seal
Springbank	black	wax seal
Stag's Breath	black	whisky liqueur
Ye Monks	tan	wax seal

Novelties and Curiosities

Visitors to Scotland will be aware of the many novelty containers of whisky that are offered for sale in tourist shops. These novelties vary greatly in quality but nearly all have in common the fact that the whisky content is largely irrelevant. Among the best of the figures are the wildlife models originally produced by  Wades for Peter Thompson Ltd of Perth, but now marketed by Whyte & Mackay. At one time Peter Thompson sold 'The Thistle and the Rose' chess set, based on personalities from Scottish and English history.

Bell's decanter in the shape of a hand bell is found in various capacities, including 5cl. The company presented employees with a miniature bell, to commemorate the wedding of the Prince of Wales; this ceramic container is rare enough to command the highest asking price of any miniature whisky.

Ceramic novelties have come in a variety of shapes, from footballs to curling stones and from bulls to books. A list of those most likely to be found in Scottish shops is given in the following page.

Another curiosity is the micro-mini or piccolo. One firm in Scotland markets these with various proprietary labels. There is an entry in the Guinness Book of Records to substantiate the claim that these are the smallest bottles of whisky in the world.

Miniatures have been sold in combined packs with other products from tartan dollies to marmalade and shortbread. More appropriately, some malts have been sold along with a glass for tasting. Bowmore was one of the first in this field, with a large thistle-shaped glass in an elaborate pack. Isle of Jura, Bruichladdich, Deanston and Tullibardine followed; Glenmorangie's elegant tasting glass is provided with a little lid to hold in the aroma!

Some years ago, the 'family pack' was a popular souvenir. Bells, MacDonald & Muir, Dewars, Morrison's Bowmore, Mackinleys and Glenlivet Distillers all marketed such samplers of their product ranges.

Here is a selection of miniature novelties found in many Scottish shops:

Container Shape	Issued By	Notes
Hand Bell	Bells	tan, paper label
Curling Stone	Glen Calder	
Whisky Still	Glen Calder	10cl
Whisky Measure	Macphails	copper or pewter
Golf Club Head	McGibbons	
Whisky Barrel	Rutherfords	
Book (several colours)	Rutherfords	"Spirit of Scotland"
Bull	Rutherfords	brown
Mac (head of Scot)	Rutherfords	tan
Kilted Scot	Rutherfords	
Thistle	Rutherfords	
Golf Ball	St Andrew's	
Tennis Ball	St Andrew's	
Badger	Whyte & Mackay	Originally
Squirrel	Whyte & Mackay	issued by
Otter	Whyte & Mackay	Peter
Seal	Whyte & Mackay	Thompsons Ltd
Golden Eagle	Whyte & Mackay	of Perth
Grizzly Bear	Whyte & Mackay	
Loch Ness Monster	Whyte & Mackay	
Haggis	Whyte & Mackay	
Whisky Barrel	Whyte & Mackay	

Springbank also sold book-shaped miniatures, containing different ages of their malt.

Displaying Miniatures

Whatever its size, a collection of miniatures can provide a fine feature display. A small collection is easy enough to accommodate but, as more bottles are accumulated, dusting becomes a problem and some sort of enclosed cabinet is desirable. Any glass-fronted display shelving may be adapted but a larger collection will justify having cabinets specially made by a local joinery firm.

Only another 112 to go.................

Lengths of 40mm x 40mm timber can be used to economise space in shelving. Six cut to the required length will give four tiers on a 150mm wide shelf. With a gap of 300mm between shelves, this arrangement will permit the display of 100 miniatures per metre of shelving. A more sophisticated system may be devised, using 50mm wide plate glass instead of the timber.

DISPLAY STAND MADE FROM SIX 1½" BATTENS

Vatted Malt Miniatures

George Sainsbury, whose 'Notes on a Cellar-Book' is a connoisseur's classic, would blend different malts in various ways, the better to enjoy the flavours; a mixture of Clynelish and Glenlivet is one he approved. Such 'do-it-yourself' vatting has not caught on. The current proprietory brands of vatted malts are probably designed for the less adventurous palate and seek to provide a malt that is consistent in flavour. As such they are best regarded as an extension of the practice of vatting various casks from a single distillery to obtain a 'standard' taste. With the increased popularity of the single malts and the new-found willingness to promote them, the vatted kind is now much less in evidence than hitherto.

The four 'Prides' issued by Gordon & MacPhail, are interesting in that they give an opportunity to taste vatted malts on a regional basis.

'Own Label' Malts

It is sometimes impossible to distinguish a vatted malt from a single malt that has been put out under the bottler's own label. Both may be referred to as 'pure malt' or 'all malt'. Where the source of an 'own label' malt is specified (and not, as some are, simply implied) on the label, it is listed along with the single malts. The rest are lumped together under the heading 'Vatted and Own Label Malts' on page 77.

Single Grain Whisky Miniatures

Two single grain whiskies are marketed by the proprietors: Haig's Choice Old Cameron Brig and Invergordon. The launch of the latter included a miniature. 5cl 'samplers' of Caledonian and Cameron Brig have been available very briefly on 'open days' at the distilleries. There have been merchant's miniatures of Strathmore (North of Scotland), Dumbarton and North British Grain Whiskies. A list is found on page 78.

Whisky Liqueurs

During the eighteenth and early nineteenth centuries, local whisky was found in few genteel Scottish homes; ale, wine and brandy were more likely to be used. The practice of maturing whisky in wood to remove the harsher elements was not widespread and the raw product of the Highland stills was largely left to ordinary folk. However, it was found that the rough edge of immature whisky could be disguised by adding fruits, herbs and other flavourings. The toddies and punches that resulted from this discovery are forerunners of the present-day whisky liqueurs.

The first whisky based liqueur to be marketed, and still the most familiar, is Drambuie. The romantic tale of its association with the wanderings of Prince Charles Edward is told on the label. In common with liqueurs the world over, the formulation of Drambuie is a closely guarded secret but it has been followed by several with a similar theme: Glayva, Chivas Brother's Loch an Ora, Loch Lomond, and Gordon & MacPhail's Atholl Brose all appear to depend on honey for their characteristic flavours.

Two of the latest introductions are Oran Mor and Stag's Breath. Both are stylishly packaged; the latter indicates the inclusion of fermented comb honey among its ingredients. The label on Glenturret Malt liqueur states that herbs are added but does not identify the source of its sweetness.

The origins of Atholl brose are lost in early highland history. Brose is prepared by pouring boiling water or milk onto oatmeal; whisky would be a natural additive! However, the liqueur now available is 'Meg Dodd's Dunkeld Atholl Brose' and contains no oatmeal.

Inspired, perhaps, by the success of Bailey's Irish Cream, a couple of rather similar concoctions have been marketed in Scotland – Heather Cream and Columba Cream. Quite different is Mrs McGillivray's Apple liqueur, which is marketed by the same company as Drambuie.

All the liqueurs mentioned above have been sold in miniature form. A list appears on page 76.

Single Malt Whiskies

The making of malt whisky has been described succintly by Birnie (1939), as follows:

> "Clean barley is turned into Malt by Steeping, Germination and Drying. It is then Mashed with hot water, to produce a sweet solution of Malt Extract. Fermentation with Yeast turns to sugar into Alcohol. Distillation is then carried out twice in Pot Stills. The resulting raw Malt Whisky is put into wooden casks to mature."

Each stage in the production of a particular malt whisky helps the formulation of its unique character. The extent to which peat is used in malting, the source of the process water, the shape of the stills, the selection of the middle cut of each distillation, the type of cask used, the conditions under which it is stored and the duration of the maturation process, will all have bearing on the taste of the malt whisky when finally it is committed to the bottle. When thus bottled, without the addition of a grain whisky (which would make a blend) or of a whisky from another malt distillery, it is termed a single malt or, in older parlance, a self whisky.

There are 117 malt distilleries in Scotland whose product might be available for bottling. Some 33 of these were dismantled or mothballed during the eighties. A total of 104 different malts have been put into miniature bottles by the proprietors or by independent merchants, though not all are currently available.

Using Malt Whisky Miniatures as Samplers

with Apologies to Glen Grant ....

The collector who is not a whisky drinker may be content to place his single malt miniatures on a shelf with the rest. The whisky drinker who enjoys tasting whisky's equivalent to the Château wines, will have a better use for them. He will welcome the increasing availability of these miniatures because they make it easier to sample the products of many distilleries without the expense of a full bottle, in surroundings of his own choosing.

The Age of Malt Whisky

The age of most bottled malt whiskies is stated on the label. As whisky matures only in the wood, the age is that at the date of bottling. Whisky distillers consider that there is a certain age when each malt reaches a peak of maturity, after which that malt will not improve. The age may vary greatly from one malt to another but there seems to be a general agreement that Speyside malts reach his peak at about 15 years.

For the connoisseur, the age of a single malt may be of quite profound importance. He will tell you that two whiskies from the same distillery but different ages can vary significantly in taste. Indeed, he may discern between an eight year old and a 15 year old Glen Grant a wider variation of tasting experience than between a Glen Grant and a Glenlivet of the same maturity.

Details of age are not always given on the label but the absence of this information does not necessarily indicate extreme youth. Some companies, seeking a wider market for their malts will value consistency of taste, obtained by mixing different ages of their malt, above commitment to a certain vintage. Examples of single malts with no age on the label are Glen Grant and Glenfiddich.

The oldest whisky made available in bottle is a 1919 Springbank. A limited edition appeared in shops in 1985. Less than two dozen miniatures were bottled, all with numbered labels. There have been 75cl bottlings

of 50 year old Macallan, Dalmore, Balvenie and Mortlach; only the latter has appeared in miniature form, with a stylish Gordon & MacPhail label. This firm has also issue miniatures of their similarly aged 'Pride of Strathspey' and 'MacPhail's' malts; wording on the labels suggests that both are single malts, perhaps from the same distillery.

Glenlivet and the Definite Article

When such things mattered more than they do today, the chief of one Highland clan declared that only three people were entitled to place 'The' before their name: The King, The Pope and The Chisolm.

Prefixing the definite article to suggest primacy is a device used to promote several malt whiskies. In recent advertising, Macallan has gone further and styled itself 'The Malt'. All right for Macallan, but when applied to lesser malts,'The' has about the same connotation as 'Finest' has on the label of so many blended whiskies.

One distillery has gained recognition in law for a 'The' before its name. Smith's Glenlivet distillery had the distinction of being the first to take out a licence under the Whisky Act of 1823. Their whisky gained a great reputation in Victorian times and other distillers sought to share its fame by adding 'Glenlivet' to their own name. A lawsuit in 1880 failed to stop this but did win George and J G Smith the sole right to the title 'The Glenlivet'. The continuing use of the name by others, led to advertisements like this:

> "George and John Gordon Smith ... beg to intimate that **Glenlivet** is a district which belongs to his Grace the Duke of Richmond and Gordon, and that their Distillery was the **first** and is now the **only** licensed Distillery in Glenlivet and that they are the Sole Manufacturers of 'Glenlivet Whisky'.

There are now two other distilleries in the glen and one, Tamnavulin-Glenlivet is bottled as a miniature. Seven other miniature malts have 'Glenlivet' on the label, so also has one blend, Glen Calder, which announces itself as being 'from the Glenlivet District'.

More About Proof

If you have no hydrometer and no gunpowder, it may
be handy to know another (safe) way to test the
strength of a spirit. There used to be a special container
called a 'Proof phail', but a miniature can be used for
the purpose. The method is to shake the bottle violently
and observe the characteristics of the bubbling that
results. Bubbles are larger, greater in number and
persist longer when the proof is higher. The reader may
care to experiment with miniatures of the same malt
but in different strengths.

There is little consistency among the pundits
regarding the ideal strength at which malt whisky
should be enjoyed. If one is involved in a tasting
session, comparing different malts or different bottlings
of the same malt, then a degree of dilution is usually
suggested. It is said of some malts, notably Highland
Park and Talisker, that they will taste better if diluted
from 57% to 40% at the time of tasting, than if taken
neat from a 40% bottling.

Some experts say that the usual bottling strength of
40% is too low for malt whisky tasting. Before the first
world war, the practice had been to bottle at 75° (43%)
but the lower strength was imposed in order to
economise grain usage. Most malts are bottled for
export at 43% and an increasing number now appear at
the higher strength in the UK.

There, is a body of opinion that favours drinking
malt whisky at cask strength, particularly as an after-
dinner tipple. There is now sufficient variation in
strength of miniatures in the shops to provide scope for
much experimentation!

Merchant Bottling of Malt Whisky

In the early days of the industry, the bottling of malt whiskies was undertaken by merchants and not by the proprietors of the distilleries. The practice has almost disappeared. Some of the merchants, like Teachers and Chivas Brothers have become blenders and bottlers with a large market. Others have ceased to bottle. Gordon & MacPhail continue to act as authorised bottlers on a small scale but such major distilleries as Glen Grant, Macallan and Glenlivet now directly control this aspect of their business. The change is one result of the greater emphasis now placed on the sale of single malts and the desire of the marketing companies to have a consistent product.

The character of the whisky from any distillery undoubtedly varies from cask to cask, so that it is not possible to guarantee that the malt taken from any one cask will have the particular character desired by the proprietor. The official bottler may wish to 'lose' the contents of lesser casks in his standard product, but in doing so, he will surely also lose some very good ones. It is the enthusiast who seeks the special experience of sampling a malt from a particularly fine cask who will be the customer of a new breed of Merchant bottlers. These merchants purchase casks on the open market and bottle the contents, using their own brand name, but indicating the distillery of origin on the label.

Among the first to offer this kind of bottling to the general trade was Wm Cadenhead. Gordon & MacPhail followed with their distinctive 'Connoisseur's Choice' label. Others in the field are Prestonfield House, Signatory Vintage and James McArthur & Co. The products of these firms will be found in specialist whisky shops; all of them issue miniatures which serve as excellent introductory samplers to what is now a very wide range of malt whiskies at interesting ages and in a variety of strengths.

Glen Grant and Gordon & MacPhail

The firm of Gordon & MacPhail has had a long and distinguished connection with the whisky trade, in particular as bottlers of fine malts. They were also pioneers in the bottling of miniature Scotch whiskies. In the thirties they bottled the first Glen Grant miniatures in pear-shaped bottles, corked and capsuled. After the war, they introduced the flask miniature which was later put into the now familiar tartan carton with acetate front. This 'Tartanpak' range, purchased as souvenirs and gifts, has introduced malt whisky into thousands of homes.

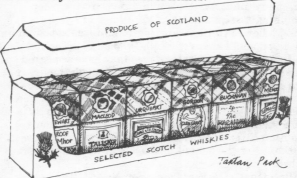

Gordon & MacPhail have bottled many distinguished malt whisky miniatures and they have broken new ground with, for example, the series for the two royal weddings. They have 5cl versions of their bottlings of 50 year old Mortlach, 'MacPhail's' and 'Pride of Strathspey' and they have issued the oldest blended whisky in miniature form – 40 year old Glen Calder, with a fine picture label.

The Connoisseurs Choice selection has made available for tasting many of the SMD malts that had previously gone entirely for blending. The series also provides the opportunity to taste Glencraig and Mosstowie and to compare these products of Lomond stills with standard malts from Glenburgie and Miltonduff respectively.

Wm Cadenhead's Miniatures

William Cadenheads were Aberdeen merchants who had their own blends and bottled some malts, including Laphraoig and Ardbeg, with uniform black labels. Since the firm moved its operating base to Campbeltown, where it is closely associated with Springbank, they have bottled the products of many other distilleries, some at unusual ages, using the same kind of label.

In 1979, Cadenheads issued a set of twelve miniatures all at 80° proof, including a unique bottling of St Magdalene, a lowland distillery now converted into housing. This was the first time that well matured malts – Highland Park and Mortlach both at 22 years old – were made available in a form convenient for sampling. A second batch of 12, all aged 17 years or more, followed in 1983. Further miniatures appeared in specialist retail shops in 1986, 1988 and 1990.

In addition to the miniatures that have appeared on general sale, others have been sold through the firm's own outlets in Edinburgh and Campbeltown. These have included some limited editions, perhaps re-filled from 75cl bottles, with rather dull labels that do little more than state the contents: these are costly items and have little significance except for the compulsive collector. For the benefit of the latter, the limited issues include:

Balmenach (19 years old), Ben Nevis (19), Caol Ila (16), Cardow (=Cardhu) (16), Cragganmore (15), Glen Elgin (15), Glenkinchie (21), Glenlivet (30), Glenlossie (18), Glen Mhor (21), Ladyburn (14), Lagavulin (13), Longmorn (26), Macduff (13), Mortlach (16), North Port (17), Oban (21), Ord (25), Port Ellen (15), Royal Brackla (18), Scapa (26), Talisker (21), Tamnavulin (18) and Teaninich (26).

This was the first bottling in miniature of Ladyburn and Teaninich malts.

Other Unofficial Bottlings

The miniature bottled by James McArthur & Co all contain malts at twelve years of age and all are at cask strength. The labels are uniform in appearance but the information given is particularly clear. Along with the more usual details, the cask numbers are shown but not the year in which they were filled. All MacArthurs miniatures are also found in standard size bottles and are issued primarily as samplers.

Also bottled at cask strength were the two malts, Balvenie and Macallan, marketed by Macfarlane Bruce and Co, Inverness, under their 'As We Get It' label. The age of the malt is not stated.

The selection of casks by merchants sometimes appears erratic. In the case of Signatory Vintage, there is also a confusing variety in the strength at which bottling is carried out. The information given on the labels is very full and each one is hand numbered. This firm's list includes two Single Grain Whiskies: North British and Dumbarton.

The Scotch Malt Whisky Society also bottles malts obtained on the open market. The purchase of casks appears to be more selective and purposeful than is the case with merchants. Full-sized bottles are filled at cask strength and are sold only to members. From time to time the society also fills miniatures, but at reduced strength. Their purpose is to enable members to sample new issues before deciding to buy a large bottle. The miniatures may not be purchased by non members of the Scotch Malt Whisky Society. Few of the society's bottlings state the name of the distillery, though the provenance of the malt is usually fairly obvious from the details given in the prospectus.

Tasting Malt Whiskies – Miniatures as Samplers

The purpose of this section is to help the person who has tasted only a few malts chart his way through the bewildering variety now available, using miniatures as the most convenient way to obtain samples. Praise for particular malt whiskies abounds in the 'connoisseur' literature and no attempt is made to add to it. The aim is to make it easier for the reader to arrive independently at his own 'Top Ten' list.

Tasting malt whiskies is not an activity to be carried out alone. The first requirement, therefore, is one or two boon companions with the same general experience of tasting.

QUANTITIES: One 5cl miniature is ample for at least two tastings, if several malts are to be sampled in a session and if judgement is to remain unimpaired throughout.

TASTING GLASS: Any glass will do but sometime try one of the tulip-shaped similar to the blender's nosing glass.

WATER: A little water added before tasting is said to release the aroma. It is not necessary unless you want to weaken the whisky. If your tap water is likely to add taste as well, use a bottled water, like 'Highland Spring'.

REFERENCE MALT: To help comparisons, it may be useful to introduce one particular malt into most tasting sessions. Better to choose a run-of-the-mill malt rather than one with strong individuality.

NOTEBOOK: If you are serious about tasting, a record made at the time of sampling will be invaluable for future comparisons. Such a record may help in selecting a few meaningful descriptive words which may later serve as a defence against the extraordinary catalogue of tasting terms found in whisky literature.

Tasting Experience

It may seem odd to make suggestions about how to taste malt whisky, but these notes may be useful, even if only to help understand the fine distinctions drawn by others. The sampling of a malt is carried out in three stages:

Nose:
The aroma or bouquet. A sort of reconnaisance by sniffing. This is how the blender judges the whiskies he samples. (He might be hard put to actually taste 750 specimens of whisky in a day).

Palate:
The taste in the mouth where the flavour is decided. If a wine were the subject of the tasting, this might be the end of it and the sample might be spat out. Fortunately, there is a further stage in the tasting of malt whisky, which requires that the spirit be swallowed.

Throat:
After the warm feeling in the throat comes the 'aftertaste' or 'aftermath' – a reprise of taste, in which the expert may detect elements missed by nose or palate.

Tasting Areas:
The usual classification of malts into Highland, Lowland, Campbeltown and Islay leaves a disproportionately high number of malts in the highland category. For this reason, the latter has been divided into six, so that we have nine tasting areas, as follows:

1. Lowland
2. Campbeltown
3. Islay
4. Other Island
5 Northern Highland
6. Southern Highland
7. Speyside
8. Keith & Elgin
9. Eastern Highland

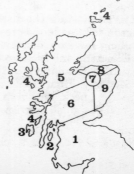

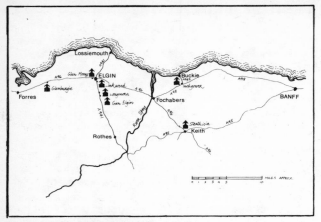

Keith & Elgin

Banff, Benriach, Benromach, Coleburn, Dallas Dhu, Glenburgie (also Glencraig), Glencadam, Glendronach, Glen Elgin, Glen Keith, Glenlossie, Glen Moray, Inchgower, Knockdhu, Linkwood, Longmorn, Macduff, Miltonduff (also Mosstowie), Royal Brackla, Strathisla.

The Keith & Elgin distilleries produce malts with many characteristics in common with their Speyside neighbours. A number are still labelled Glenlivet, a classification to be cautious of, being perhaps as unreliable as a guide to taste as it is to geographical location.

The product of Macduff distillery is bottled officially (though not yet in miniature) as Glen Deveron, after the river on which the distillery stands. Dallas Dhu no longer produces but is preserved as a museum. Banff distillery has been dismantled.

Glencraig and Mosstowie are the names applied to particular distillations at Glenburgie and Miltonduff respectively. Final distillation is in stills with a short cylindrical neck, known as 'Lomond' stills after the original design at Inverleven.

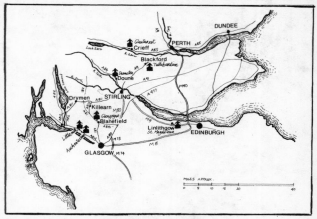

Southern Highlands

Aberfeldy, Ben Nevis, Blair Athol, Deanston, Edradour, Glengoyne, Glen Lochy, Glenturret, Loch Lomond, Oban, Tullibardine.

The characteristic taste of these malts is said to reflect their geographical position between the Lowlands and the Highlands proper, with bias towards the former. Oban and Blair Athol are exceptions, being described as 'smokey'. Ben Nevis is the first Scotch whisky distillery to be owned by a Japanese whisky company. The malt from Loch Lomond distillery is marketed as 'Inchmurrin'.

Lowland Malts

Auchentoshan, Bladnoch, Glen Flagler, Glenkinchie, Kinclaith, Littlemill, Rosebank, St Magdalene.

Some malt whisky drinkers scorn the Lowland malts as being too slight for serious tasting. However, they should be sampled; their lightness and want of 'aftermath' may in fact be very acceptable to the drinker who prefers not to be browbeaten by his whisky – or by the pundits! Glen Flagler, Kinclaith (both formerly located within a larger grain distilling complex) and St Magdalene have been dismantled.

45

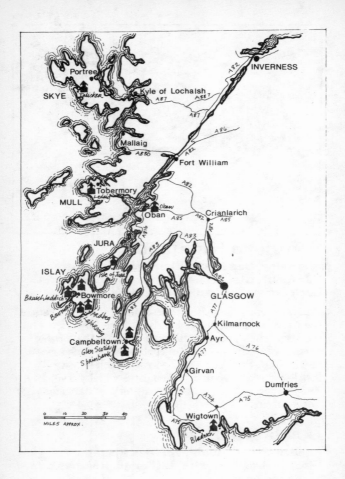

Campbeltown

Glen Scotia, Springbank (and Longrow).

If the art of distilling came to Scotland from Ireland,
then Campbeltown, only a few miles from Antrim coast,
is surely the birthplace of Scotch whisky.

There have been as many as 32 distilleries in the
Campbeltown area when these malts were in great
demand for blending. Economic depression and a
failure to maintain standards led to mass closures in
the late 1920s. Only Springbank survived in continuous
production; its stills have also been used to produce a
distinctive whisky from a strongly peated malt which is
bottled as 'Longrow'. The whisky from Glen Scotia,
which has produced intermittently since being revived
in 1933, is said to be closer than Springbank to the
Campbeltown malts of earlier days.

Isle of Islay

Ardbeg, Bowmore, Bruichladdich, Bunnahabhain, Caol Ila, Lagavulin, Laphraoig, Port Ellen.

Powerful, pungent, peaty, full-bodied, medicinal and
tasting of seaweed, antiseptic or iodine: These are some
of the words used to describe Islay's malts. Whatever
you think of the distinctive 'Islay' taste, unless you
have sampled and savoured the varied characteristics
of these malts, you only half know Scotch whisky.

· Laphroaig ·

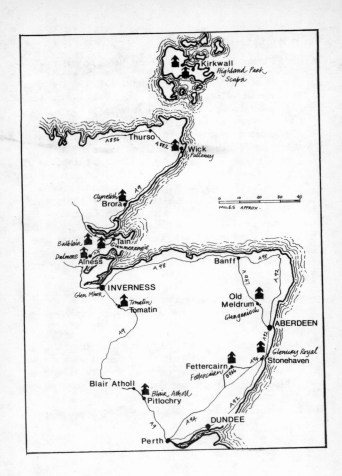

Kirkwall
Highland Park
Scapa

A836 Thurso
A882 Wick
Pulteney

Clynelish A9
Brora

Balblair Tain
G.Glenmorangie
Dalmore
Alness
A98 Banff A98

Glen Mhor INVERNESS A941 A72

Tomatin Old
Tomatin Meldrum
Glengarioch ABERDEEN

A9 A92
Glenury Royal
Fettercairn A94 Stonehaven
Fettercairn B966

Blair Atholl
Blair Atholl A92
Pitlochry A94 DUNDEE
A9
Perth

0   10   20   30   40
MILES APPROX.

Eastern Highland

Fettercairn, Glen Esk, Glengarioch, Glenury, Glenugie, Lochnagar, Lochside, North Port.

The malts from the eastern part of the highland area are reputed to be gentler than those of Speyside but more characterful than those from further south. Individuality of character is well illustrated by Glen Garioch (those in the know say 'Geerie'), an earlier bottling of which was described as having 'a magnificent robust nose, flowery, not very smoky; it is surprisingly mild on the palate ...' This example of tasting prose does not originate from a panel of malt whisky experts, but from the bottlers own publicity.

Northern Highland

Balblair, Clynelish, Dalmore, Glen Albyn, Glen Mhor, Glenmorangie, Glenordie (Ord), Millburn, Pulteney, Tomatin.

The great difference in reported tasting characteristics between Clynelish ('full flavoured', 'like Laphraoig') and Glenmorangie ('fragrant', 'mellow') illustrates the hazzard of grouping malts into tasting areas. Exceptions like this serve to remind us that every single malt has its own individual character.

Other Island

Highland Park, Isle of Jura, Tobermory (Ledaig), Scapa, Talisker.

Like the islands themselves, these are malts of great individuality. Tobermory single malt is available only as 'Ledaig' in a Connoisseur's Choice bottling. Highland Park is found in a variety of strengths and its reputation when well matured can also be tested from the range of available miniatures.

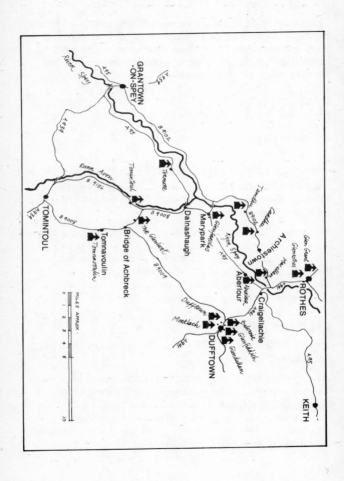

GRANTOWN
-ON-SPEY

River Spey

A95

A939

A95

B9102

River Avon

Tomintoul

Tormore

B9136

TOMINTOUL

A939

B9008

B9008

Dalnashaugh

Marypark

Tomnavoulin

Tomnavoulin

Bridge of Achbreck

The Glenlivet

B9009

Tamdhu

Cardhu

Knockando

River Spey

A95

Glenfarclas

Aberlour

Aberlour

A941

Craigellachie

Tamnavulin

Glen Grant

Glenrothes

ROTHES

A95

Dufftown

Mortlach

Fiddich

DUFFTOWN

Balvenie

Glenfiddich

Glendullan

A95

KEITH

MILES APPROX.

0 1 2 3 4 6 10

Speyside

Aberlour, Auchroisk, Balmenach, Balvenie, Benrinnes, Caperdonich, Cardhu, Convalmore, Cragganmore, Craigellachie, Dailuaine, Dalwhinnie, Dufftown, Glenallachie, Glenfarclas, Glenfiddich, Glen Grant, Glenlivet, Glenrothes, Glentauchers, Imperial, Knockando, Macallan, Mortlach, Pittyvaich, Speyburn, Tamdhu, Tamnavulin, Tomintoul, Tormore.

Although they offer a wide variety of tasting experience, the Speyside malts belong together as a group, none standing out strongly as having characteristics more typical of another area. These are the classic malt whiskies of Scotland.

One of the phenomena of malt whisky can be experienced by sampling miniatures of Glenfiddich and Balvenie; these sister distilleries, with common ownership and drawing water and malted barley from the same source, differ noticeably in taste. Both use casks of varying ages in their bottling and it has been claimed for Balvenie that use of a high proportion of whisky matured in sherry casks has influenced the flavour. Macallan sets even greater store by the benefits of maturation in casks that have been used previously for the storage of sherry.

Faced with a problem of pronunciation, the proprietors of Auchroisk (the locals refer to 'A'thrusk') distillery labelled their product 'The Singleton', a term hitherto seldom found away from the bridge table. (A similar problem was solved at Auchentoshan by calling the product 'Glen Toshan' in some markets. More boldly, marketing men at Highland Distillers have made a selling point of the difficulty non-gaelic speakers may have in saying 'Bunnahabhain'.)

Malt Distilleries and Associated Blends

Macallan and Genfarclas are two independent distilleries whose products are prized by blenders but which cannot be linked directly to any particular brand. Most other distilleries are owned by or are closely connected with firms whose principal activity is the production and marketing of one or more brands of blended whisky. The smaller groups will purchase malts from outside sources, so that in some cases, the company's own malt may not be dominant in the blend.

Distillers Company ... United Distillers

The Scotch whisky industry has been dominated for over 60 years by the conglomerate DCL and its successor, United Distillers. The latter is a subsidiary of Guinness PLC who, having absorbed Arthur Bell & Sons in 1986, took control of Distillers Company in 1987. Before the takeover, the group's distilling activities were largely controlled through Scottish Malt Distillers and Scottish Grain Distillers, though individual distilleries remained associated with certain constituent companies of DCL, like Buchanan's, White Horse and Johnnie Walker.

Distillery	Associated Brand
Aberfeldy, Ord	Dewars
Balmenach	Crabbies, Peter Dawson
Banff (closed)	Thistle, Lord Douglas
Benrinnes	Crawford's 5 & 3 Star
Bladnoch, Blair Athol Dufftown, Inchgower	Bells Real Mackenzie
Caol Ila	Bulloch laid, Old Rarity
Cardu, Talisker	Johnnie Walker
Clynelish	Ainslie's Royal Edinburgh
Coleburn	Usher's, Jamie Stuart
Convalmore, Dalwhinnie Glentauchers (sold)	Buchanans, Black & White House of Commons, Royal Household
Cragganmore	McCallum's Perfection
Craigellachie, Glen Elgin, Lagavulin	White Horse
Glendullan	Old Parr

Distillery	Associated Blend
Glen Esk	VAT 69
Glen Kinchie, Glenlossie, Manochmore	} Haig
Glenury Royal	King William IV
Dallas Dhu (sold)	Benmore
Knockdhu (sold)	King of Kings
Linkwood	Abbot's Choice, Chequers
Lochnagar	John Begg
Millburn (closed)	Macleay Duff
Mortlach	John Barr
Oban	Old Mull
Rosebank	King George IV
Royal Brackla	Bisset's
Teaninich	Robbie Burns

Others in the group: Aultmore, Benromach, Brora (closed), Dailuaine, Glen Albyn (closed), Glenlochy, Glen Mhor (closed), Imperial (sold), North Port, Port Ellen, St Magdalene (closed) and Speyburn.

Allied Distillers
Owners of the second largest group of malt distilleries and incorporating Hiram Walker and Long John Distillers: The purchase of Imperial and Glentauchers from United Distillers brought their total to fifteen.

Milton Duff, Inverleven	
Ardbeg, Balblair, Scapa	} Ballantine's
Pulteney, Glenburgie	Old Smuggler
Ardmore, Glendronach	Teachers
Glencadam	Stewart's Cream of the Barley
Glenugie, Laphraoig	} Islay Mist
Tormore, Kinclaith	Long John

Seagram Distillers
Largest producers of alcoholic drinks in the world, they established themselves in the UK market by buying Chivas Brothers in 1949. They then purchased two distilleries and built two more. The takeover of Glenlivet Distillers in 1978 brought the total of malt distilleries under Seagram's ownership to nine:

Glen Keith, Strathisla,	Passport, 100 Pipers
Allt a' Bhainne, Braes of Glenlivet	Chivas Regal, Royal Salute

Benriach, Longmorn,
Glenlivet, Glen Grant,
Caperdonich

Queen Anne, St Leger
Something Special

Invergordon Distillers have six distilleries:
Ben Wyvis, Deanston
(both closed),
Bruichladdich, Jura,
Tamnavulin, Tullibardine

Primarily producers for
others, but they market
Scots Grey and Glenfoyle

Highland Distillers and associated companies:
Bunnahabhain, Glen
Rothes,Highland Park,
Tamdhu
Glengoyne

Famous Grouse,
Cutty Sark

Langs Supreme

Pernod Ricard
Aberlour, Glenallachie
Edradour

Clan Campbell, White
Heather, King's Ransom,
House of Lords

William Grant & Sons
Balvenie, Glenfiddich,
Ladyburn, Kininvie

Grant's,
Grant's Royal

IDV (Gilbey Vintners):
Knockando, Auchroisk
Glen Spey, Strathmill

J & B Rare, Royal Ages,
Catto's, Spey Royal

Whyte & Mackay:
Three of their own distilleries contribute to Whyte &
Mackay blends: Dalmore, Fettercairn and Tomintoul.

Stanley P Morrison:
Operate three distilleries: Auchentoshan, Bowmore and
Glengarioch. Their Rob Roy blend is familiar to
miniature collectors and they have many export
brands.

Macdonald & Muir:
Their best known malt, Glenmorangie, is not used in
blending but Glen Moray contributes to the taste of
Highland Queen, Muirheads and James Martin blends.

Limited Editions and Rare Malt Miniatures

The rarest miniature whiskies are survivors from an age when these bottlings were samples for use, which nobody would think to preserve. There are several examples of miniatures from 'Milton Distillery' (name changed to Strathisla in the early fifties), including a pear-shaped bottle which is possibly the oldest malt miniature surviving with contents intact.

More modern rarities command greater attention from collectors. There is a miniature containing 60 year old Scotch bearing a Buchanan's label. It is known to be a sample of Royal Brackla, taken from a limited shipment to Japan in 1986. This scarce item is on public display with the rest of Derek Taylor's collection in Thurso. Also on view there is a miniature of 15 year old Ardmore, specially bottled by teachers for a 'Children in Need' appeal. For the same cause, five miniatures of 50 year old Mortlach, with suitably annotated labels, were auctioned in 1988. The only previous 5cl bottling of Ardmore was done by Cadenheads for the Mini Bottle Club.

Some Springbank malt, distilled in 1919, was rebottled in miniature form and issued in a numbered edition of 23 in the mid eighties. The original bottling in December 1970 was at 66.3° proof. Some of the 1952 distillation from the same source appeared in an edition of about 40 miniatures in 1989. In the following year, Signatory Vintage marketed 30 miniatures, numbered and signed, of 1949 Macallan at a strength of 37.9% vol.

Limited bottlings by Cadenhead are listed on page 40. Some Prestonfield and all Signatory Vintage labels are numbered, but in quite large editions.

Some curious malt miniatures have turned up in very small quantities. Some may be spurious but most are thought to be trial runs or trade samples:

Altmore: There are two labels on record: a plain one, showing neither age nor strength but issued officially in the US, is illustrated in Triffin. The second, with a label in the style of the current 75cl issue, has not been released commercially.

Glen Deveron: There was a small run for the French market: it is described on the label as 'unblended Scotch malt whisky from the Macduff Highland distillery'. The only other miniature from Macduff is the 1975 Connoisseur's Choice.

Glenfarclas: A miniature of the handsome 25 year old bottling has appeared, apparently without the knowledge of the owners of the distillery.

Glendronach: There are small numbers of both 8 and 12 year old Glendronach in two versions; one has facsimile labels, the other plain.

Macallan: In 1979, the proprietors of Macallan took over direct responsibility for the bottling of 'The Finest Single Malt Whisky on Speyside'— (to quote the label). The occasion was marked by the issue of a miniature with an odd spiral label, which specifies neither the age nor the strength of the contents.

Glenglassaugh: Another mysterious miniature originating in Italy, where a limited number of 75cl bottles had been marketed by Highland Distillers.

Blair Athol, Dufftown: These two malts were sold in some markets at 12 years old; a few miniatures, given away at trade fairs, have found their way back to this country. The labels are in the 'coat of arms' style of the eight year old miniatures sold here.

Recent advances in techniques of photocopying make it easy to reproduce in miniature the label of a 75cl bottle. Collectors should therefore be wary of 'true' miniatures that have no known history!

The Mini Bottle Club

Collectors of miniature whiskies wishing to know more about their hobby and who seek contact with others with a similar interest, may wish to join the Mini Bottle Club, the only such organisation in the United Kingdom. Details may be obtained by sending a stamped addressed envelope to the membership secretary:

> David Hamilton
> 47 Burradon Road
> Burradon
> CRAMLINGTON
> NE23 7NF

The club covers all liquors found in small bottles, but the main focus of attention is on scotch whisky. There is a bi-monthly newsletter which covers all aspects of collecting; it includes illustrations of new issues and has had some useful in-depth profiles of some brands. *(See pages 75 & 94)*

Members of the Mini Bottle Club hold periodic 'House Meetings' in many areas. These social gatherings are the occasion for the exchange of information and the swapping of bottles.

Triffin

An important source of information for collectors is the American publication *The Whiskey Miniature Bottle Collection* by James A Triffin. Volume 2 covers Scotch whisky and illustrates most of the miniatures issued in the United States from the end of prohibition up to 1981.

Derek Taylor's Collection

Travellers to the remote north of Scotland will find this important collection at the Royal Hotel in Thurso. It is one of the most complete collections of miniature Scotch whiskies and the only one on public display.

Hunting Miniature Whiskies

Miniature whiskies may legally be sold from premises that are licensed for off-sales. In Scotland, such licences do not permit sales on Sundays.

The miniatures listed in this book will be found in retail shops. Some of the specialised outlets are given opposite. Even these shops will not have discontinued brands in stock long after they cease to be issued. Indeed, one is more likely to find old issues in smaller shops, off the beaten track.

Two places where the miniature hunter is least likely to buy, are distilleries that do not have a Visitor Centre (and this means **most** distilleries) and the sales offices of blending companies. Even where distilleries have their own shops, it is as well to remember that their main business is to produce whisky, not to sell it in small bottles!

Another point to remember is that if you cannot find a particular miniature in a specialist shop, the supplying blender will have exhausted his stocks long before. Besides, even though they handle millions of bottles each year, a blender's own premises is itself unlikely to hold an off-sales licence.

A Mini Whisky Hunter and Dog

When writing for information to a distillery or a blending company, or for a price list to a shop, it would be a courtesy to enclose a stamped addressed envelope for the reply.

Hunting Whisky Miniatures – A Buyer's Guide

Most off-licence stores stock miniatures of the popular brands only. The traveller in Scotland will find shops with a good range of miniatures in most tourist centres but there are only a few outlets with really comprehensive stocks where you are likely to get knowledgeable help from the proprietor or his assistants. There follows a list of retail establishments that are known to offer a good service for the collector. Some publish lists and offer a mail order facility:

SCOTLAND

Aboyne, Aberdeenshire – George Strachan & Co, licensed grocers in the Station Square. Specialists with plenty of miniatures including many old labels. They also have their own Wild Oats, Uisge Beatha, Pheasant Plucker, etc.

Inverdruie by Aviemore, Inverness-shire – Cairngorm Whisky Centre has an excellent stock of miniatures and full size bottles. There is also a tasting room with a whisky museum and video show. Open all year.

Edinburgh – Lambert Brothers, Frederick Street, just off Princes Street. Old established wine merchants with a strong whisky section and a fine stock of miniatures, some unobtainable elsewhere. Their own bottlings include Arthur's Seat, Heather, Howtowdie and Robert the Bruce.

– The Whisky Shop, Waverley Market. A busy, crowded little shop whose good stock includes its own 'Mist' series.

– Cadenheads, in the Royal Mile, has a very small selection of miniatures but some may be exclusive to them.

Elgin, Morayshire – Gordon & MacPhail, South Street. Long established merchants and bottlers of fine malt whiskies. They have a very wide range of miniatures in stock.

Pitlochry – Highland House in the main shopping centre has a large stock of novelties as well as miniatures. Closed November, January and February.

Tomintoul – The Whisky Castle has an excellent selection of whiskies, both 75cl and miniature.

Glasgow – The Whisky Shop, Princes Square
Tyndrum – Clifton Craft Centre
Oban – Cheese and Wine Shop
Fort William – Scottish Craft Centre
Four good stockists of miniature whiskies in the west.

There are few miniature specialists in England but the following have excellent stocks:

Blackpool – 'The Wee Dram', 5 Queens Square, is a mecca for collectors of miniatures and figurines from all parts of the world.

Lincoln – The Whisky Shop, Bailgate are specialists with good miniature stocks.

London – Harrods, Knightsbridge, have all the usual miniatures plus, exclusively, a few of their own.
– The Whisky Shop, Sedgwick Centre, Aldgate Bars, a branch of the Edinburgh Whisky Shop.

Further Reading

There is an ever growing body of literature on the subject of Scotch whisky. In seeking information, the reader needs to be wary because there have been many changes in structure and ownership, especially during the eighties. However, the process of making whisky has hardly changed and some straightforward accounts are to be found in the publicity literature of the major companies.

Although some of the earlier studies of the industry are no longer of much interest to the present-day reader, the following have attained the status of classic: Sir Robert Bruce Lockhart – *Scotch, The Whisky of Scotland in Fact and Story* (Putnam). This is a warm and very personal study by a man who had his roots in Speyside.

Neil Gunn – *Whisky & Scotland* (Souvenir Press)

J Marshall Robb – *Scotch Whisky* (Chambers, 1950) is a delightful book; it describes itself as the first illustrated guide to whisky and is worth reading for the foreword by Maurice Walsh and for George Mackie's drawings.

Two more up-to-date general guides are:
Michael Brander – *The Essential Guide to Scotch Whisky* (Canongate, 1990)

J Wilson – *Scotland's Malt Whiskies* (Famedram, 1990)

For the briefest of surveys, try:
Susan Fleming – *The Little Whisky Book* (Piatkus, 1988)

An anthology of words and pictures from the past comes from the pen of the most articulate of modern whisky writers: Derek Cooper – *A Taste of Scotch* (Andre Deutsch, 1989). His *Companion to Whiskies* (Century) remains one of the best reference books for the general reader.

Although the original edition of 1983 is now out-dated, Philip Morrice – *The Schweppes Guide to Scotch* (Alphabooks) is still a most useful directory of the whisky industry, in its commercial aspects.

To discover the character of a malt whisky, few

people need do more than taste a sample. There has been a rash of writing recently that suggest that this is not enough. It may be advisable to get the opinion of an expert taster first! There has always been a temptation for writers to pontificate a little about their favourite malts but a new trend was set by *Decanter* magazine whose *Harrods Book of Whiskies* details the findings of a panel of four expert tasters on practically all available malts. So, for the reader who does not quite trust his own judgement, here is a choice of three oracles:

Michael Jackson – *Malt Whisky Companion* (Dorling Kindersley) – his *World Book of Whisky* is a comprehensive survey including whiskies other than Scotch.

Wallace Milroy – *Malt Whisky Almanac* (Lochar)

John Lamont – *The Malt File* (Benedict Books)

Finally, the most comprehensive survey of the Scotch whisky scene, fully annotated and well illustrated:

Michael S Moss & John R Hume – *The Making of Scotch Whisky*. This book is a worthy successor to Alfred Barnard's classic *The Whisky Distilleries of the United Kingdom* (originally published in 1887, reprinted by Mainstream in 1987 and also, covering surviving Scottish distilleries only, by Famedram).

The Future for Miniature Whiskies

The whisky trade is never static and the supply of miniatures is always changing. Familiar label may disappear but new ones appear to fill the gap. Collectors constantly seek out new labels and it is hoped the demand generated by this expanding hobby will help to persuade the whisky companies to further develop this aspect of their promotional activities. The more miniatures that are produced by the traditional whisky trade, the less scope there will be for those fringe operators who may appear on the scene to take advantage of the constant demand for new labels.

An increasing number of malt whisky producers have become aware of the benefits that can come from making miniature bottles of their products available for tasting. A further widening range of 'samplers' will be pleasing to that growing band of knowledgeable people who find malt whisky tasting an agreeable occupation and who would like to broaden the spectrum of their experience.

There is still some scope for the development in the sphere of 'own label' bottlings and this will be welcomed by those collectors who travel widely in pursuit of new labels. Easy access to cheap printing will further encourage the use of miniatures to commemorate special events, for fund raising and for product promotion.

Several distilling firms have been willing to make their malts available for use with special labels. It is to be hoped that this trend will continue and that promoters will thus be encouraged to pay attention to the contents of the miniature as well as to the label!

Blended Whisky Miniatures – Explanation of Lists

The blended whiskies listed in the following pages are those miniatures that were available for purchase in the UK at the time of writing.

NAME OF BLEND This is the name most prominent the label. The name of the bottler is given only when it is part of the name

DETAILS Age is shown if it is on the label. Proof is noted only when the label indicates that strength is different from the standard 40% vol

SHAPE
T	True Miniature *(see page 12)*
Ro	Round – standard tall
Rd	Round – dumpy style
Sq	Square, tall – also known as 'Irish Square'
Sd	Square – dumpy style
Fa	Flat – standard 'airline', rounded edges
Fl	Flask – curved, hip flask style
Fs	Flat – rectangular section
Tri	Triangular in section
Dec	Decanter or decorative bottle
Var	Issued in a variety of formats

COLOUR Cl Clear   Bl Black   Br Brown   Gr Green

NOTES
TP	'Tartanpak' format from Gordon & MacPhail
DL	Issued by Douglas Laing & Co
GS	Issued by Gordon Strachan, Aboyne
LB	Issued by Lambert Brothers, Edinburgh
SC	Marketed by Scottish Collection, Edinburgh
WS	Issued by Whisky Shop, Waverley Market
GM	Bottled by Gordon & MacPhail
Pres	Prestonfield

Blended Whisky Miniatures

Name of Blend	Age	% vol	Avail		Shape/Colour		Notes
Abbot's Choice			+	–	Cl	Fa	Boxed
Aberdeen Mist			++	–	Cl	Ro	WS
Aboyne Games			++	–	Cl	Ro	GS
Ainslie's Royal Edinburgh			+	–	Br	Fa	Boxed
Airlie Castle			++	–	Cl	Ro	Pres
Ambassador de Luxe			+	T	Cl	Ro	
Ambassador	12yo	43%	+	T	Cl	Ro	
Antiquary	12yo		+	T	Cl	Dec	
Argyll			++	T	Cl	Sq	
Arisaig Mist			++	–	Cl	Ro	WS
Arthur's Seat			++	–	CL	Ro	LB
Auchinloch			+		Var		DL
Auld Curlers			+	–	Cl	Ro	GS
Auld Reekie			++	–	Cl	Ro	LB
Auld Rorie			++	–	Cl	Ro	LB
Auld Skye			++	–	Cl	Ro	SC
Avonside		40%	++	–	Cl	Fl	GM also TP
Avonside		57%	++	–	Cl	Fl	GM TP
Backpacker's Blunder			++		Cl	Ro	SC
Balgownie			+	T	Cl	Ro	GS
Ballantine's			++	T	Cl	Fs	
Ballantine's	12yo	43%	++	T	Cl	Fs	
Barley Bree			++		Cl	Ro	LB
BB Gold			+		Var		DL
BB Red			+		Var		DL
Bell's			++		Cl	Dec	
Bell's Islander			++	T	Cl	Ro	
Bell's	12yo		++	T	Cl	Ro	
Bell's	21yo		++	T	Cl	Dec	
Ben Alder			++	T	Cl	Ro	GM also TP
Beneagles			++	T	Cl	Ro	
Ben Nevis Mist			++	T	Cl	Ro	WS
Ben Roland			++		Cl	Ro	

Blended Whisky Miniatures

Name of Blend	Age	% vol	Avail	Shape/Colour			Notes
Big T			++	T	Cl	Ro	
Black & White			++	T	Cl	Ro	
Black & White	12yo		+		Cl	Ro	
Black Bottle			++	T	Gr	Dec	
Black Colt			++		Cl	Ro	LB
Black Douglas			+		Var		DL
Blair Castle			++		Cl	Ro	Pres
Bottoms Up			++		Cl	Ro	SC
Boulevard			++		Cl	Ro	LB
Brahms & Liszt			++		Cl	Ro	SC
Bridges			++		Cl	Ro	LB
Brodick Castle			++		Cl	Ro	Pres
Brodie's Supreme			+		Cl	Ro	
Buchanan's Blend	8yo		++	T	Cl	Ro	
Buchanan's Reserve	12yo		+		Cl	Ro	
Buckie Lugger			++		Cl	Ro	GS
Cairn's			+	T	Cl	Sq	
Caledonia			++		Cl	Ro	LB
Callandar Mist			++		Cl	Ro	WS
Campbeltown Loch			++	T	Cl	Ro	
Capital Dram (Edinburgh)			++		Cl	Ro	SC
Carlton	5yo		++		Cl	Fl	
Catto's			+	T	Cl	Ro	
Cheetah Chaser			++		Cl	Ro	WS
Chequers			++	T	Cl	Ro	
Chieftain's Consort			++		Cl	Ro	SC
Chivas Regal	12yo		++	T	Cl	Rd	
Christmas Newt			++		Cl	Ro	WS
Clan Blend			+	T	Cl	Ro	GM also TP
Clan Campbell	5yo		++	T	Cl	Ro	
Clan Campbell	12yo		++	T	Cl	Ro	
Climber's Cure			++		Cl	Ro	SC
Cluny	5yo		+		Cl	Fa	
Clydebank			++		Var		DL
Clydebank Centenary			+		Cl	Ro	
Cockburn's OV8			++		Cl	Fa	
Commonwealth Games			+		Cl	Ro	
Cotton's No 1			++		Cl	Ro	LB

Blended Whisky Miniatures

Name of Blend	Age	% vol	Avail	Shape/Colour			Notes
Craigievar Castle			++		Cl	Ro	Pres
Craiglieth			++		Cl	Ro	LB
Crathes Castle			++		Cl	Ro	Pres
Crawford's ***			++		Cl	Fa	
Cream of the Barley (Stewart's)			++	T	Cl	Dec	
Crinan Canal Water			++	T	Cl	Ro	
Culzean Castle			++		Cl	Ro	Pres
Crown of Scotland			+	T	Cl	Ro	
Cutty Sark			.++	T	Cl	Ro	
Dad's Dram			++		Cl	Ro	SC
Dalmeny			+		Cl	Fl	
Davaar			++	T	Cl	Ro	
Deerstalker			++		Cl	Ro	LB
Dewar's Ancestor			+	T	Cl	Sd	
Dewar's White Label			++	T	Cl	Ro	
Dice			+		Var		DL
Dimple Haig	12yo		+	T	Cl	Dec	
Dimple Haig	15yo		++	T	Cl	Dec	
Director's Choice			++		Cl	Ro	LB
DL13			+		Cl	Var	
Duck Bay			++		Cl	Ro	
Drumnadrochit Dram			++		Cl	Ro	SC
Dunhill Old Master			++	T	Cl	Dec	
Durham Mist			++		Cl	Ro.	
Eaglesome's			++	T	Cl	Ro	
Eaton's			++		Cl	Var	DL
Edinburgh Mist (9 different labels)			++			Ro	WS
Eight Fellows			++		Var		DL
Eilean Donan Castle Mist			++		Cl	Ro	WS
Eilean Donan Dram			++		Cl	Ro	SC
Emblem			++		Cl	Ro	SC
Falcon			++		Cl	Ro	
Famous Grouse			++	T	Cl	Ro	GS
Findlater's Finest			++	T	Cl	Ro	
Finest Liqueur			+		Cl	Fa	
Forth Bridges			++		Cl	Ro	LB
Forth Bridge Centenary			++		Cl	Ro	LB
Fraser Supreme			++		Cl	Ro	GM

Blended Whisky Miniatures

Name of Blend	Age	% vol	Avail	Shape/Colour		Notes
Gael Lonach			++		Cl Ro	GS
Gairloch			+		Cl Fa	
Glamis Castle			++		Cl Dec	Boxed
Glasgow Mist (2 labels)			++		Cl Ro	WS
Glen Calder			++		Cl Ro	GM also TP
Glen Calder	40yo		++	T	Cl Ro	GM
Glen Calder		57%	++		Cl Fl	GM TP
Glenfinnan Mist			++		Cl Ro	WS
Glen Garry			++		Cl Ro	LB
Glen Ghillie			++		Cl Ro	LB
Glen Guard			+		Var	DL
Glen Lindsay			++		Cl Ro	LB
Glenmorrison Old Farm			++	T	Cl Ro	
Glen Niven			+	T	Cl Ro	
Glen Piper			++		Cl Ro	LB
Golden Lion			+	T	Cl Ro	
Golfer's Tee			++		Cl Ro	SC
Gouden Drappie			++		Cl Ro	LB
Grand McNish			++	T	Cl Ro	
Grant's Family			++	T	Cl Tri	
Grant's	12yo		++	T	Cl Tri	
Grant's Royal	12yo		+	T	Cl Tri	
Grendel's	12yo		+		Cl Fa	DL
Grog Blossom			++		Cl Ro	GS

Blended Whisky Miniatures

Name of Blend	Age	% vol	Avail	Shape/Colour			Notes
Haig's Gold Label			++	T	Cl	Ro	was Fl
Hamilton			+		Var		DL
Hart's			+		Cl	Fa	DL
Headington			++		Cl	Ro	LB
Heather			++		Cl	Ro	LB
Heebie Jeebies			++		Cl	Ro	GS
Hielanman			+		Cl	Ro	old label
Hielanman	8yo		++		Cl	Ro	
Highland Fusilier 25 anniversary			+	T	Cl	Ro	GM also TP
Highland Haze			++		Cl	Ro	LB
Highland Mist			+	T	Cl	Ro	
Highland Mist	8yo		+	T	Cl	Ro	
Highland Queen			++	T	Cl	Ro	
Highland Sporran			++		Cl	Ro	
House of Lambert			++		Cl	Ro	LB
House of Lords	8yo		++	T	Cl	Sd	Older Fl
House of Lords	12yo		+	T	Cl	Sd	
House of Peers			++		Var		DL
House of Stuart			++	T	Cl	Ro	2 labels
House of Strachan			++		Cl	Ro	GS
Howtowdie			++		Cl	Ro	LB
Hundred Pipers			++	T	Cl	Ro	
Immortal Memory			++		Cl	Ro	
Imperial Gold Medal (Cockburn's)			+	T	Cl	Ro	
Imperial (Watson's)			+		Cl	Fa	
Inebriated Newt			++		Cl	Ro	WS
Inver House			++	T	Cl	Ro	
Inverness Mist			++		Cl	Ro	WS
Isle of Skye	8yo		++	T	Cl	Fs	
Isle of Skye	12yo		+	T	Cl	Fs	
Isle of Skye	18yo		++	T	Cl	Fs	
Isle of Skye Mist (2 labels)			++		Cl	Ro	WS

Blended Whisky Miniatures

Name of Blend	Age	% vol	Avail	Shape/Colour			Notes
J & B Rare			++	T	Cl	Ro	
J & B	15yo		++	T	Cl	Rd	Boxed
James Martin	VVO		++	T	Cl	Ro	
James Martin	12yo		+	T	Cl	Ro	
John O'Groats			++	T	Gr	Dec	
John Barr			++	T	Cl	Sq	
John Player Special			++	T	Cl	Sq	DL
Johnnie Walker Black			++	T	Cl	Sq	
Johnnie Walker Red			++	T	Cl	Sq	
Kentshire			+		Var		DL
Keswick Mist			++		Cl	Ro	WS
Kindrochit Castle			++		Cl	Ro	GS
King of Scots			++		Var		DL
King's Ransom			+		Cl	Fl	
King William IV			++	T	Cl	Ro	
Lakeland			++		Cl	Ro	SC
Lambert's Favourite			++		Cl	Ro	LB
Langside			+		Var		DL
Lang's Select	12yo		+	T	Cl	Dec	
Lang's Supreme			++	T	Cl	Ro	
LBE Black			++		Cl	Ro	LB
LBE Red			++		Cl	Ro	LB
Leland's			++		Cl	Ro	LB
Linlithgow Mist			++		Cl	Ro	WS
Liverpool Garden Festival			+		Cl	Ro	
Lochinver Blend			++		Cl	Ro	SC
Lochlomac			+		Var		DL
Lochgilphead			++		Cl	Ro	
Loch Ness Mist			++		Cl	Ro	WS
Logan de Luxe			+		Cl	Fs	
Lombard's			++		Cl	Fl	
London Mist			++		Cl	Ro	WS
Long John			++	T	Cl	Ro	
Lord Douglas			++	T	Cl	Ro	
Lothian Pride			++		Cl	Ro	LB
Lucky (Black Cat)			++		Cl	Ro	SC

Blended Whisky Miniatures

Name of Blend	Age	% vol	Avail	Shape/Colour			Notes
MacArthur's			+	T	Cl	Ro	
McCrae's Blend			+		Cl	Var	DL
McGibbons			+		Cl	Var	DL
Mackinlay's Original			++	T	Cl	Ro	
Mackinlay's Legacy	12yo		++		Cl	Ro	
Mackinlay's	12yo	43%	++		Cl	Fa	Gold
Mackinlay's	21yo		++	T	Cl	Ro	
Macphail's Special	5yo		++	T	Cl	Ro	GM also TP
Mac's Delight			++		Cl	Ro	LB
Master of Arts			++		Cl	Sq	Also 8, 12yo
Maxim's			+		Cl	Fa	PET
Maxim's	12yo		+	T	Cl	Ro	
Moidart			++	T	Cl	Sq	
Moncreiffe	8yo		++		Cl	Ro	
Mons Meg			++		Cl	Ro	LB
Monster's Choice			++	T	Cl	Ro	GM
Monument			++		Cl	Ro	LB
Morrison's Machrie	8yo		++		Cl	Ro	
Morton's			++	T	Cl	Ro	
Morton' Special Reserve			+	T	Cl	Ro	
Mother's Toddy			++		Cl	Ro	SC
Muirheads			+	T	Cl	Ro	
Munros (various names)			++		Cl	Ro	LB
Murdoch's	15yo		++		Cl	Fa	PET
Murnane's			++		Cl	Ro	LB
National Choice			++	T	Cl	Ro	
Nessie's Nip			++		Cl	Ro	SC
New Year Newt			++		Cl	Ro	WS
Nick's Nip			++		Cl	Ro	LB
Nick (Shepherd's Friend)			++		Cl	Ro	SC
Nicky Tams			++		Cl	Ro	LB
Nine & Eleven			++		Cl	Ro	LB
Noble Glen			+		Cl	Var	DL
Noble Highlander			++		Cl	Ro	SC
Notorious Ptarmigan			++		Cl	Ro	SC

Blended Whisky Miniatures

Name of Blend	Age	% vol	Avail		Shape/Colour		Notes
Old Arthur			+		Cl	Fa	
Old Barrister			+		Cl	Ro	
Old Cobblers			++		Cl	Ro	GS
Old Court			++		Cl	Ro	
Old Highland Liqueur			++		Cl	Ro	LB
Old Inverness			++	T	Cl	Ro	
Old Orkney			++	T	Cl	Ro	GM also TP
Old Parr			+	T	Br	De	Boxed
Old Rarity	12yo		+	T	Cl	De	
Old Royal	15yo		++		Cl	Fa	
Old Scotia			++		Cl	Ro	LB
Old Smuggler			+	T	Cl	Ro	
Old Smuggler	12yo		+	T	Cl	Ro	
Old Tarbet			++		Cl	Ro	SC
Old Troon			+		Cl	Ro	
Old Troon Royale			+		Cl	Ro	
Panda's Potion			++		Cl	Ro	WS
Parliament Mist			++		Cl	Ro	WS
Pheasant Plucker			++	T	Cl	Ro	GS
Pig's Nose			++	T	Cl	Ro	
Pinwinnie			++		Cl	Fa	
Plockton Mist			++		Cl	Ro	WS
Prestonfield House			++	T	Cl	Ro	Boxed
Prime Blend			++		Cl	Ro	LB
Prince			+		Cl	Sq	
Prince Howard			++		Cl	Ro	
Puffin's Pleasure			++		Cl	Ro	SC
Putachieside			++		Cl	Ro	
Queen Anne			++	T	Gr	Ro	
Ram's Dram			++		Cl	Ro	SC
Rambler's Rescue			++		Cl	Ro	SC
Real Mackenzie			++	T	Cl	Ro	
Red Gauntlet			++		Cl	Ro	
Robbie Burns			+	T	Br	Dec	
Robert the Bruce			++		Cl	Ro	LB

Blended Whisky Miniatures

Name of Blend	Age	% vol	Avail	Shape/Colour			Notes
Rob Roy			++	T	Cl	Ro	
Rochambeau			++		Cl	Ro	LB
Rock Hopper Tipple			++		Cl	Ro	WS
Ronson	5yo		+	T	Cl	Sq	
Ronson	12yo		+	T	Cl	Sq	
Royal Deeside			++	T	Cl	Ro	GS
Royal Findhorn			++	T	Cl	Ro	GM
Royal Wee			++		Cl	Ro	SC
Sandy MacNab			+		Cl	Fl	
Sandy MacNeil			++		Cl	Ro	LB
Saunders			+		Cl	Var	DL
Scotch House	8yo		+		Cl	Fa	PET
Scotch Select			++		Cl	Ro	LB
Scotch No 10	(Acredyke's)		++	various			Dl
Scotia Royale	12yo		++	T	Cl	Ro	
Scotland's For Me!			+		Cl	Ro	
Scottie			++		Cl	Ro	LB
Scottish Choice			++		Cl	Ro	LB
Scottish Gourmet			+	T	Cl	Ro	
Scottish Reel			++		Cl	Ro	LB
Scots Grey			+		Cl	Fa	
Seventy Seven			++	various			DL
Shieling			++		Cl	Ro	LB
Sir Walter Raleigh			++	various			DL
Skipper			+	various			DL
Slaintheva			++		Cl	Ro	
Souvenir			++		Cl	Ro	
Spey Cast			++	T	Cl	Ro	GM also TP
Spey Cast	12yo		++		Cl	Fl	GM TP
Spirit of the MacDonalds			++		Cl	Ro	SC
Spirit of Scotland			++		Cl	Ro	SC
Steaming in the Highlands			++		Cl	Ro	SC
Stirling Mist			++		Cl	Ro	WS
Stuart Royal	8yo		++	T	Cl	Ro	

Name of Blend	Age	% vol	Avail	Shape/Colour			Notes
Talisman			++		Cl	Ro	LB also Fa
Tammie			++		Cl	Ro	LB
Tappit Hen			++		Cl	Ro	LB
Tax Collector			++	T	Cl	Ro	
Teacher's			++	T	Cl	Ro	
Teacher's 60			++	T	Cl	Ro	
Teacher's Christmas			++		Cl	Ro	Boxed
Teviotdale			+	T	Cl	Ro	
Thistle			+	T	Cl	Ro	
Three Brothers			++		Cl	Ro	LB
Tight Lines (Angler's Dram)			++		Cl	Ro	SC
Tinker's Dram			++		Cl	Ro	GS
Tobermory			++		Cl	Ro	
Tourist's Torment			++		Cl	Ro	SC
Turnberry Reserve			++		Cl	Ro	
Turnbull's Club			+	T	Cl	Ro	
Tuxedo			++		various		DL
Ubique			++	T	Cl	Ro	GM
Uisge Beatha			++	T	Cl	Ro	GS
Uist Mist			++		Cl	Ro	WS
Union Park			++		Cl	Ro	LB
Vat 69			+	T	Gr	Dec	
Wee Windaes			++		Cl	Ro	LB
Westminster Mist			++		Cl	Ro	WS
Whisky of 1990			++	T	Cl	Ro	
White Hart			+		Cl	Ro	
White Heather	5yo		+	T	Cl	Sd	
White Horse			++		Cl	Fl	
White Horse America's Cup			+	T	Cl	Fs	
Whiteinch			++		various		DL
Whyte & Mackay			++		Cl	Fa	
Whyte & Mackay de Luxe			+	T	Cl	Fa	
Whyte & Mackay	21yo		++	T	Cl	Dec	Boxed
Wild Oats			++		Cl	Ro	GS
William Lawson			++	T	Cl	Ro	
York Mist			++		Cl	Ro	WS
Zebra Zelect		46%	++		Cl	Ro	WS

Notes

The newsletters of the Mini Bottle Club have contained occasional articles on the miniatures of individual brands. The following is a list of the blended whiskies that have been profiled:

Antiquary–May '87; Ambassador–July '88;
Black Bottle–January '89; Douglas Laing–March '90;
Cream of the Barley–November '89; Red Hackle–March '88;
Rob Roy–September '88

Scotch Whisky Liqueurs

Brand	Age	% vol	Avail	Shape/Colour			Notes
Atholl Brose		35	++	T	Gr	Rd	GM
Columba Cream		17	++		Br	Fl	
Drambuie		40	++	T	Br	Rd	
Glayva		35	++	T	Cl	De	
Glenturret		35	++		Cl	Ro	
Heather Cream		17	++	T	Br	De	
Hot Toddy		28.5	+		Cl	Fa	
Lochanora		35	+	T	Br	Sd	Chivas
Oran Mor	12 yo	40	++	T	Gr	Ro	Boxed
Scotch Apple		25	++	T	Gr	Rd	
Stag's Breath		19.8	++		Cl	Fa	

Vatted Malt Whiskies
Own Label Malt Whiskies

This list covers only those miniatures that are available currently in retail shops. For an explanation of the list, see page 79.

Campbeltown Commemorative	12	40	+		Cl	Ro	24 different names
Dalchully	15	40	+	T	Cl	Ro	'Speyside'
Dewar's Malt	12	43	+	T	Cl	Ro	
Drover's Dram		40	++		Cl	Ro	
Fisherman's Friend		40	++		Cl	Ro	
Glen Avon	8	40	++	T	Cl	Ro	GM
Glen Avon	25	40	++		Cl	Ro	GM
Glencoe	8	57	++		Cl	Fl	
Glen Gordon	8	40	++		Cl	Ro	GM
Golfer's Dram		40	++		Cl	Ro	
Highland Fusilier	8	40	++	T	Cl	Ro	GM also TP
Highland Fusilier	8	60	+		Cl	Ro	GM
Highland Fusilier	12	40	++	T	Cl	Ro	GM
Highland Fusilier	15	40	++	T	Cl	Ro	GM
Inchmurrin		40	++	T	Cl	Ro	
Macphail's	10	40	++	T	Cl	Ro	GM
Macphail's Islay	10	40	++	T	Cl	Ro	GM
Macphail's	1965	40	++	T	Cl	Ro	GM
Macphail's	1964	43	+	T	Cl	Ro	GM
Macphail's	1938	40	++	T	Cl	Ro	GM
Macphail's Royal Wedding	26	40	++	T	Cl	Ro	GM A&S
Macphail's	50	40	++		Cl	Ro	GM
Macphail's	10	57	++		Cl	Fl	GM TP
Mar Lodge	12	43	++	T	Cl	Sd	
Old Elgin	8	40	++	T	Cl	Ro	GM
Poit Dhubh	12	40	++	T	Cl	Ro	
Prestonfield Islay	1965	43	++	T	Cl	Ro	Bowmore
Prestonfield Islay	1972	43	++	T	Cl	Ro	Bowmore
Prestonfield Campbeltown	1967	46	++	T	Cl	Ro	S'Bank
Prestonfield Highland	1970	43	++	T	Cl	Ro	
Pride of Islay	12	40	++	T	Cl	Ro	GM also TP
Pride of the Lowlands	12	40	++		Cl	Fl	GM TP
Pride of Orkney	12	40	++	T	Cl	Ro	GM also TP
Pride of Orkney	12	57	++		Cl	Fl	GM TP
Pride of Strathspey	12	40	++	T	Cl	Ro	GM also TP
Pride of Strathspey	25	40	++		Cl	Fl	GM TP
Pride of Strathspey Royal Wed	26	40	++	T	Cl	Ro	GM A&S
Pride of Strathspey	50	40	++		Cl	Ro	GM
Sheep Dip	8	40	++		Cl	Ro	
Speyside	8	43	++		Cl	Fa	PET
Strathayr		43	+		Cl	Ro	
Strathconon	12	40	++	T	Cl	Ro	
Whisky Trail		40	++		Cl	Ro	

Note: Only a few of the Campbeltown Commemorative titles remain on retailer's shelves. Longrow, one of the distillery names included in the series is also used by Springbank to identify a particular variation of its product.

Single Grain Miniatures

Distillery	Age	% vol	Avail-ability	Shape		Bottled by	Notes
Caledonian		40			Cl Fl	Prop	see page 31
Cameron Brig		40		T	Cl Ro	Prop	see page 31
Dumbarton	1961	46	++		Cl Ro	SV	
Invergordon	10	43	++	T	Cl Ro	Prop	
North British	1964	46	++		Cl Ro	SV	
Strathmore	1964	57	+		Cl Ro	GS	North of Scotland

Single Malt Whisky Miniatures Explanation of Lists

DISTILLERY: The name of the distillery is almost always the name on the label. Exceptions are: Glencraig (Glenburgie), Ledaig (Tobermory), Longrow (Springbank) and Mosstowie (Miltonduff). In the lists, use of 'The' before the distillery name is ignored, even for The Glenlivet.

AGE AND PROOF: as stated on the label. If known, but not shown on the miniature label, details are put within brackets.

AVAILABILITY: ++ currently widely available in UK
                       + Older issue, still found in some shops
On the lists, where a miniature will not be found in any shop, the entry is indented.

SHAPE: Ro Round, standard   Rd Round, dumpy
              Sq Square, tall   Sd Square, dumpy
              Fa Flat, airline   Fl Flask, curved
              Fs Flat, square section   Tri Triangular
              De Decanter, decorative
              T   True Miniature (see page 12)

COLOUR: Cl Clear Bl Black   Br Brown   Gr Green

AREA: See Tasting Guide (page 43)

NOTES   Cad   Bottled by Wm Cadenhead (see page 40)
              G&M Bottled by Gordon & MacPhail (see page 39)
              cc   Connoisseurs Choice label from G&M
              TP   'Tartanpak' format from G&M
              McA   Bottled by James McArthur & Co
              SV   Signatory Vintage bottling
              Pres Prestonfield House bottling
              Prop Bottled by the propietor of the distillery

Some variations in labelling cannot easily be described in words. To aid identification, where labels have been illustrated in Triffin (see page 57) or in the Mini Bottle Club Newsletters (see page 57), the fact is indicated by the abbreviation Tr or MBC in the notes.

Malt Miniatures

Distillery	Age/Proof		Avail-ability	Shape & Colour			Area	Bottled by	Notes
Aberfeldy	1974	40	++	T	Cl	Ro	South	G&M	cc map
Aberfeldy	1969	40	+	T	Cl	Ro		G&M	cc old
Aberfeldy	1970	40	+	T	Cl	Ro		G&M	cc both
Aberfeldy	1966	40		T	Cl	Ro		G&M	cc old
Aberlour	10	40	++	T	Cl	Ro	Spey	Prop	Castle label
Aberlour	12	40	+	T	Cl	Ro		Prop	Castle label
Aberlour	1970	46	++		Cl	Ro		SV	
Aberlour	12	43		T	Gr	De		Prop	VOHM
Aberlour	12	40		T	Cl	Sd		Prop	
Aberlour	10	43		T	Gr	De		Prop	VOHM France
Aberlour	8			T	Cl	Sd		Prop	Tr Italy also Ro
Aberlour	9	70		T	Cl	Sd		Prop	Tr also Fa
Ardbeg	1976	40	++	T	Cl	Ro	Islay	G&M	cc map
Ardbeg	1973	46	++	T	Cl	Ro		SV	
Ardbeg	15	46	++		Cl	Ro		Cad	
Ardbeg	1975	40	+	T	Cl	Ro		G&M	cc map
Ardbeg	1974	40	+	T	Cl	Ro		G&M	cc both
Ardbeg	10	(70)	+		Cl	Fl			
Ardbeg	17	46	+		Cl	Ro		Cad	
Ardbeg	1973	40		T	Cl	Ro		G&M	cc old
Ardbeg	1977	40		T	Cl	Ro		G&M	cc old
Ardbeg	10	(70)		T	Gr	Ro		Prop	also Fl
Ardbeg	10	80			Gr	Ro		Prop	Tr
Ardbeg	14	80			Gr	Ro		Cad	
Ardbeg		80			Gr	Ro			MBC88 light lbl
Ardmore	21	46	+		Gr	Ro	East	Cad	
Auchentoshan	5	40	++	T	Cl	Ro	Low	Prop	buff label
Auchentoshan	10	40	++	T	Cl	Ro		Prop	also 43
Auchentoshan	12	40	++		Cl	Fa		Prop	also Ro
Auchentoshan	(5)	40		T	Gr	Ro		Prop	dark label with scene
(Glentoshan)	(5)	40			Cl	Fa		Prop	MBC88 buff lbl
(Glentoshan)	(5)				Cl	Fa		Prop	Tr Italy
Auchroisk	1976	40	++	T	Cl	Ro	Spey	Prop	'Singleton'
Auchroisk	1975	40	++	T	Cl	Ro		Prop	'Singleton'
Auchroisk	12	59.3	++		Gr	Ro		Cad	
Aultmore	12				Cl	Ro	K&E	Prop	Tr light label
Aultmore				T	Cl	Ro		Prop	MBC90 col lbl (page 56)

Malt Miniatures

Distillery	Age/Proof		Avail-ability	Shape & Colour		Area	Bottled by	Notes
Balblair	10	40	++	T Cl Ro		North	G&M	
Balblair	10	40	++	Cl Fl			G&M	TP 2 labels
Balblair	10	57	++	Cl Fl			G&M	TP 2 labels
Balmenach	1971	40	++	T Cl Ro		Spey	G&M	cc map
Balmenach	1970	40	+	T Cl Ro			G&M	cc old
Balvenie	10	40	++	Gr Dc		Spey	Prop	
Balvenie	1974	43	++	Cl Ro			SV	
Balvenie	1973	46	+	Cl Ro			SV	
Balvenie		40	+	Gr De			Prop	also 3cl
Balvenie		108.6		Cl Fa				'As We Get It'
Balvenie	8	70		Gr Fa			Prop	Tr also 43
Banff	1974	40	++	T Cl Ro		K&E	G&M	cc both
Banff	1968	40		T Cl Ro			G&M	cc old
Ben Nevis	1966	40	+	T Cl Ro		South	G&M	cc both
Ben Nevis	22	46	+	Cl Ro			Cad	
Ben Nevis	1965	40		T Cl Ro			G&M	cc old
Benriach	1969	40	++	T Cl Ro		K&E	G&M	cc both
Benrinnes	1968	40	++	T Cl Ro		Spey	G&M	cc both
Benrinnes	18	55.3	++	Gr Ro			Cad	
Benrinnes	27	44	++	Gr Ro			Cad	
Benrinnes	23	46	+	Cl Ro			Cad	
Benromach	1969	40	++	T Cl Ro		K&E	G&M	cc map
Benromach	1970	40	+	T Cl Ro			G&M	cc map
Benromach	1968	40	+	T Cl Ro			G&M	cc both
Bladnoch	8	40	++	T Cl Ro		Low	Prop	
Bladnoch		40	+	T Cl Ro			Prop	
Bladnoch	1966	43	++	Cl Ro			SV	
Bladnoch		70		T Cl Ro			Prop	MBC88 white lbl
Bladnoch	13	80		Gr Ro			Cad	Tr
Blair Athol	8	40	++	T Cl Ro		South	Prop	Pictorial
Blair Athol	8	40	+	T Cl Ro			Prop	'Coat of Arms'
Blair Athol	23	57.1	++	Gr Ro			Cad	
Blair Athol	21	46	+	Cl Ro			Cad	
Blair Athol	12			Cl Ro			Prop	'Coat of Arms'
Blair Athol	8	70		T Cl Ro			Prop	earlier neck label
Blair Athol	8	70		T Cl Ro			Prop	diff dist picture
Blair Athol	12	70		Br Ro			Prop	Tr Italy
Bowmore	10	43	++	T Cl Ro		Islay	Prop	Seagull
Bowmore	12	40	++	T Br De			Prop	also 43 also Ro
Bowmore	10	40	++	T Cl Ro			Prop	Garden Festival
Bowmore	1965	43	++	T Cl Ro			Prop	
Bowmore	11	58.4	++	Gr Ro			Cad	
Bowmore	19	46	+	Cl Ro			Cad	
Bowmore	(8)	70		T Br De			Prop	Tr
Bowmore	8	70		T Cl Ro			Prop	Ship label Tr
Bowmore	14	46		Gr Ro			Cad	
Bowmore	13	80		Gr Ro			Cad	Tr
Bowmore	7			Cl Ro			Prop	light lbl MBC88

Malt Miniatures

Distillery	Age/Proof		Avail-ability	Shape & Colour			Area	Bottled by	Notes
Bruichladdich	10	40	++	T	Cl	Ro	Islay	Prop	also 43
Bruichladdich	1970	46	+		Cl	Ro		SV	
Bruichladdich		42.9		T	Cl	Ro		Prop	also Fa
Bunnahabhain	12	40	++	T	Bk	De	Islay	Prop	in tube
Bunnahabhain	1964	46	++		Cl	Ro		SV	
Caol Ila	1974	40	++	T	Cl	Ro	Islay	G&M	cc map
Caol Ila	12	65.5	++		Gr	Ro		Cad	
Caol Ila	1975	40	+	T	Cl	Ro		G&M	cc map
Caol Ila	1969	40	+	T	Cl	Ro		G&M	cc old
Caol Ila	1972	40	+	T	Cl	Ro		G&M	cc both
Caol Ila	12	64.8	++	T	Cl	Ro		MacA	
Caperdonich	1968	40	++	T	Cl	Ro	Spey	G&M	cc both
Cardhu	12	40	++	T	Cl	De	Spey	Prop	buff label
Cardhu	12	40	+	T	Cl	Dc		Prop	oval label
Cardhu	12	40		T	Cl	Ro		Prop	pale label
Cardhu	12	43		T	Cl	Ro		Prop	Tr
Cardhu	12	43			Cl	Fa		Prop	Italy
Cardhu	8	43			Cl	Fa		Prop	Italy also T Ro
Cardow		43			Gr	Ro			France
Clynelish	12	40	++	T	Cl	Ro	North	Prop	also G&M TP Tr
Clynelish	23	51.7	++		Gr	Ro		Cad	
Clynelish	12				Cl	Fl			Tr pale label
Clynelish	5				Cl	Fl			Tr pale label
Coleburn	1965	40	++	T	Cl	Ro	K&E	G&M	cc both
Coleburn	1972	40	+	T	Cl	Ro		G&M	cc both
Convalmore	1969	40	++	T	Cl	Ro	Spey	G&M	cc both
Convalmore	26	41.6	++		Gr	Ro		Cad	
Convalmore	21	46	++		Cl	Ro		Cad	
Cragganmore	12	40	++	T	Cl	Ro	Spey	Prop	
Cragganmore	1972	40	++	T	Cl	Ro		G&M	cc both
Cragganmore	1973	40	++	T	Cl	Ro		G&M	cc map
Cragganmore	1976	40	+	T	Cl	Ro		G&M	cc map
Cragganmore	1974	40	+	T	Cl	Ro		G&M	cc map
Cragganmore	1969	40	+	T	Cl	Ro		G&M	cc old
Craigellachie	1971	40	++	T	Cl	Ro	Spey	G&M	cc map
Craigellachie	1970	40	+	T	Cl	Ro		G&M	cc map
Craigellachie	1974	40	+	T	Cl	Ro		G&M	cc map
Craigellachie	1972	40	+	T	Cl	Ro		G&M	cc both
Craigellachie	1972	46	+		Cl	Ro		SV	
Craigellachie	12	65.5	++	T	Cl	Ro		MacA	
Craigellachie	15	46	++		Cl	Ro		Cad	
Craigellachie	20	46	+		Cl	Ro		Cad	

Malt Miniatures

Distillery	Age/Proof		Avail-ability	Shape & Colour			Area	Bottled by	Notes
Dailuaine	1971	40	++	T	Cl	Ro	Spey	G&M	cc both
Dailuaine	12	62.4	++	T	Cl	Ro		MacA	
Dailuaine	23	46	++		Cl	Ro		Cad	
Dallas Dhu	10	40	++		Cl	Ro	K&E	G&M	
Dallas Dhu	1972	40	++	T	Cl	Ro		G&M	cc map
Dallas Dhu	1973	40	+	T	Cl	Ro		G&M	cc map
Dallas Dhu	1971	40	+	T	Cl	Ro		G&M	cc both
Dallas Dhu	1970	40		T	Cl	Ro		G&M	cc old
Dallas Dhu	1968	40		T	Cl	Ro		G&M	cc old
Dallas Dhu	1969	40		T	Cl	Ro		G&M	cc old
Dalmore	12	43	++	T	Cl	Ro	North	Prop	in tube
Dalmore	12	43	++		Cl	Fa		Prop	also PET
Dalmore	12	40			Cl	Rd		Prop	
Dalmore	12	(70)			Cl	Rd		Prop	
Dalmore	8	70			Cl	Fa		Prop	Macbeth
Dalwhinnie	15	43	++	T	Cl	De	Spey	Prop	also Fa
Dalwhinnie	1970	40	++	T	Cl	Ro		G&M	cc both
Dalwhinnie	1963	40		T	Cl	Ro		G&M	cc old
Dalwhinnie	15	40			Cl	Ro		Prop	pictorial label also Fa MBC66
Dalwhinnie	8	40		T	Cl	Ro		Prop	
Dalwhinnie	1962	40		T	Cl	Ro		G&M	cc old
Deanston		40	++		Cl	Ro	South	Prop	also Fa
Dufftown	10	40	++	T	Cl	Ro	Spey	Prop	pictorial label
Dufftown	8	40	+	T	Cl	Ro		Prop	'Coat of Arms'
Dufftown	8	70		T	Cl	Ro		Prop	black label
Dufftown	8	70		T	Cl	Ro		Prop	Diff dist picture
Dufftown	8				Br	Ro		Prop	Italy
Edradour	10	40	++	T	Cl	Ro	South	Prop	in tube
Edradour	1972	40	+	T	Cl	Ro		G&M	cc old
Edradour	1973	40	+	T	Cl	Ro		G&M	cc old
Edradour	1968	46	+		Cl	Ro		SV	
Edradour	18	46	++		Cl	Ro		Cad	
Edradour	21	46	++		Cl	Ro		Cad	
Fettercairn	10	43	++		Cl	Ro	East	Prop	distillery pic
Fettercairn	10	40	++		Cl	Fa		Prop	
Fettercairn	8	43	+		Cl	Fa		Prop	
Fettercairn	10	40			Cl	Rd		Prop	'Gateway' label
Fettercairn	(8)	40			Cl	Rd		Prop	
Fettercairn		70			Cl	Fl		Prop	Tartan strip
Fettercairn	(8)	(75)			Cl	Ro		Prop	'875'

Malt Miniatures

Distillery	Age/Proof		Avail-ability	Shape & Colour			Area	Bottled by	Notes
Glen Albyn	1965	40	++	T	Cl	Ro	North	G&M	cc map
Glen Albyn	1966	40	+	T	Cl	Ro		G&M	cc map
Glen Albyn	1968	40	+	T	Cl	Ro		G&M	cc map
Glen Albyn	1963	40	+	T	Cl	Ro		G&M	cc both
Glen Albyn	1964	58	++		Cl	Ro		SV	
Glen Albyn	1969	55	++		Cl	Ro		SV	
Glenallachie	12	40	++	T	Cl	Ro	Spey	Prop	also 43
Glenburgie	(20)	40			Cl	Fl	K&E	G&M	TP RW(C&D)
(Glencraig)	1970	40	++	T	Cl	Ro		G&M	cc map
(Glencraig)	1968	40	+	T	Cl	Ro		G&M	cc both
Glenburgie	5				Cl	Fa		Prop	Tr Italy
Glencadam	1974	40	++	T	Cl	Ro	K&E	G&M	cc old
Glencadam	21	46	++		Cl	Ro		Cad	
Glencraig	*see Glenburgie*								
Glendronach	12	40	++	T	Cl	Ro	K&E	Prop	'Original'
Glendronach	12	40	++	T	Cl	Ro		Prop	'Sherry Cask'
Glendronach	(26)	40	++	T	Cl	Ro		G&M	R Wed (AS)
Glendronach		70			Cl	Fl		G&M	TP
Glendronach	8			T	Cl	Ro			trade samples ⎤
Glendronach	12			T	Cl	Ro			MBC 89 ⎟
Glendronach	8	80			Cl	Ro		Prop	plain label ⎟
Glendronach	12	70			Cl	Ro		Prop	trade sample ⎦
Glendullan	12	43	+	T	Cl	Ro	Spey	Prop	
Glendullan	25	51.1	++		Gr	Ro		Cad	
Glendullan	12	47	+	T	Cl	Ro		Prop	
Glendullan	12	47		T	Cl	Ro		Prop	gold still Tr
Glen Elgin	12	43	+	T	Cl	Ro	K&E	Prop	
Glen Elgin	19	50.4	++		Gr	Ro		Cad	
Glen Elgin	14	80			Gr	Ro		Cad	Tr
Glen Esk	12	40	+		Cl	Ro	East	Prop	also 43
Glenfarclas	10	40	++	T	Cl	Ro	Spey	Prop	
Glenfarclas	1969	58.2	++		Cl	Ro		SV	
Glenfarclas	8	40	++	T	Cl	Ro		Prop	white label
Glenfarclas	21	46	++	T	Cl	Ro		Cad	
Glenfarclas	8	43		T	Cl	Ro		Prop	export
Glenfarclas	12	43		T	Cl	Ro		Prop	export
Glenfarclas	8	40		T	Cl	Ro		Prop	dark label
Glenfarclas	8	40		T	Cl	Ro		Prop	buff label
Glenfarclas	8	70			Cl	Fl		G&M	TP Tr

Malt Miniatures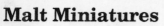

Distillery	Age/Proof		Avail-ability	Shape & Colour		Area	Bottled by	Notes
Glenfarclas	8	100		Cl	Fl		G&M	TP
Glenfarclas	8	105	T	Cl	Ro		G&M	
Glenfarclas	5	43	T	Cl	Ro		Prop	Italy also Fa
Glenfarclas	8	43	T	Cl	Ro		Prop	Italy
Glenfarclas	12	43		Cl	Fl		Prop	Tr Japan
Glenfarclas	12	104		Cl	Ro		Prop	USA
Glenfarclas	25	70		Cl	Ro		Prop	MBC89
Glenfarclas	5			Cl	Fa		Prop	'J&G Grant' Italy also no age
Glenfiddich		40	++	T Gr	Tri	Spey	Prop	
Glenfiddich	22	46	++	Cl	Ro		Cad	
Glenfiddich		70		Gr	Fa		Prop	old label
Glenfiddich	8	43		Gr	Fa		Prop	Tr
Glenfiddich	10	86US		Gr	Fa		Prop	Tr
Glenfiddich	10	43		Gr	Fa		Prop	Tr white label
Glenfiddich	8	70		Cl	Tri		Prop	Tr also Gr Ro
Glen Flagler		70		T Gr	Ro	Low	Prop	
Glen Flagler	5	40		Gr	Fa		Prop	MBC88
Glengarioch	10	43	++	T Cl	Ro	East	Prop	tube, dark label
Glengarioch	10	40	+	T Cl	Ro		Prop	box, light label
Glengarioch		70		T Gr	Rd		Prop	Tr
Glengoyne	10	40	++	T Cl	Ro	South	Prop	distillery pic
Glengoyne	10	40	+	T Cl	Ro		Prop	cream label
Glengoyne	8	70		T Gr	Ro		Prop	also Cl Tr
Glengoyne		70		T Gr	Ro		Prop	Tr
Glengoyne		70		Cl	Fa		Prop	MBC88
Glen Grant		40	++	T Cl	Ro	Spey	Prop	also 43
Glen Grant	15	40	++	T Cl	Ro		G&M	also TP
Glen Grant	12	40	+	T Cl	Ro		G&M	
Glen Grant	12	40	+	Cl	Fl		G&M	TP
Glen Grant	12	40	++	Cl	Fa		Prop	Tr
Glen Grant	26	46	+	Cl	Ro		G&M	RW A&S
Glen Grant	1964	46	++	Cl	Ro		SV	
Glen Grant	15	46	++	Cl	Ro		Cad	
Glen Grant	18	46	++	Cl	Ro		Cad	2 labels
Glen Grant	22	46	+	Cl	Ro		Cad	
Glen Grant	26	46	+	Cl	Ro		Cad	
Glen Grant	12	57	++	Cl	Fl		G&M	TP
Glen Grant	5	40		Cl	Ro			Tr
Glen Grant	20	40		Cl	Fl		G&M	TP RW C&D
Glen Grant	8	70		Cl	Fl		G&M	old TP
Glen Grant	8	100		Cl	Fl		G&M	old TP
Glen Grant	10	70		Cl	Fl		G&M	old TP Tr
Glen Grant	10	100		Cl	Fl		G&M	old TP
Glen Grant	15	70		Cl	Fl		G&M	TP
Glen Grant	15	100		Cl	Fl		G&M	TP
Glen Grant	10	70	T	Cl	Ro			Tr

Malt Miniatures

Distillery	Age/Proof		Avail-ability		Shape & Colour		Area	Bottled by	Notes
Glen Grant	10	43			Cl	Fa			Tr
Glen Grant	12	43		T	Cl	Ro			Tr
Glen Grant	16	80			Gr	Ro		Cad	
Glen Grant	20	80			Cl	Fl		Prop	age diagonal
Glen Keith	1967	46	+		Cl	Ro		SV	
Glen Keith	1963	40		T	Cl	Ro		G&M	cc old
Glenkinchie	10	43	++	T	Cl	Dc	Low	Prop	
Glenkinchie	17	46			Cl	Ro		Cad	
Glenlivet	12	40	++	T	Gr	Ro	Spey	Prop	also 43
Glenlivet	12	40	++		Cl	Fl		G&M	TP
Glenlivet	12	40	++	T	Cl	Ro		G&M	
Glenlivet	12	57	++		Cl	Fl		G&M	TP
Glenlivet	16	54.3	++		Gr	Ro		Cad	
Glenlivet	17	53.7	++		Gr	Ro		Cad	
Glenlivet	18	53.7	++		Gr	Ro		Cad	
Glenlivet	14	80	+		Gr	Ro		Cad	Tr
Glenlivet	26	46	++		Cl	Ro		Cad	
Glenlivet	1968	50.1	++		Cl	Ro		SV	
Glenlivet	50	40	++		Cl	Ro		G&M	
Glenlivet	8	70			Cl	Fl		G&M	TP
Glenlivet	8	100			Cl	Fl		G&M	TP
Glenlivet	12	45.7			Gr	Ro			Tr
Glenlivet	12				Cl	Fa			Tr
Glenlivet	18	46			Cl	Ro		Cad	Tr
Glenlivet					Br	Ro			Tr
Glenlivet			43		Cl	Fa			Tr
Glenlivet	12	91			Cl	Fa			Japan
Glenlochy	1974	40	++	T	Cl	Ro	South	G&M	cc both
Glenlochy	20	46	+		Gr	Ro		Cad	
Glenlochy	1968	40		T	Cl	Ro		G&M	cc old
Glenlochy	27	46			Cl	Ro		Cad	
Glenlossie	1969	40	++	T	Cl	Ro	K&E	G&M	cc map
Glenlossie	1970	40	+	T	Cl	Ro		G&M	cc map
Glenlossie	1971	40	+	T	Cl	Ro		G&M	cc map
Glenlossie	1968	40	+	T	Cl	Ro		G&M	cc old
Glenlossie	12	62.4	++	T	Cl	Ro		MacA	
Glenmhor	8	40	++		Cl	Fl	North	G&M	TP pink label
Glenmhor	8	57	++		Cl	Fl		G&M	TP pink label
Glenmhor	8	40			Cl	Fl		G&M	old TP
Glenmhor	8	57			Cl	Fl		G&M	old TP
Glenmhor	10	75			Cl	Ro		Prop	MBC88
Glenmorangie	10	40	++	T	Cl	Ro	North	Prop	in tube Tr
Glenmorangie	10	70			Cl	Fl		Prop	boxed Tr
Glen Moray	12	40	++	T	Cl	Ro	K&E	Prop	
Glen Moray	27	55.1	++		Gr	Ro		Cad	
Glen Moray	8	43			Cl	Ro			W Germany
Glen Moray	10	40		T	Cl	Ro		Prop	buff label Fa
Glen Moray	10	70		T	Cl	Ro		Prop	black label Fa
Glen Moray	8	40			Cl	Fa		Prop	Tr

Malt Miniatures

Distillery	Age/Proof		Avail-ability	Shape & Colour			Area	Bottled by	Notes
Glenordie			*see Ord*						
Glen Rothes	12	43	++	T	Cl	Ro	Spey	Prop	
Glenrothes	8	40	++	T	Cl	Ro		G&M	
Glenrothes	8	40	++		Cl	Fl		G&M	TP Tr
Glen Scotia	8	(40)		T	Gr	Ro	Camp	Prop	green label
Glen Scotia	5	(70)			Cl	Ro		Prop	buff label also Fl
Glen Scotia	8				Cl	Fl		Prop	Tr
Glen Scotia	12				Cl	Fl		Prop	Tr
Glen Tauchers	5	40		T	Cl	De	Spey	Prop	France MBC88
Glen Tauchers	12	43		T	Cl	De		Prop	France
Glenturret	8	40	++		Cl	Ro	South	Peop	also 43
Glenturret	12	40	++		Cl	Ro		Prop	also 46
Glenturret	10	57.1	++		Cl	Ro		Prop	
Glenturret	15	40			Cl	Ro		Prop	also 46
Glenturret	1972	40	++		Cl	Ro		Prop	
Glenturret		40	++		Cl	Ro		Prop	5000 days
Glenturret	25	52.4	++		Gr	Ro		Cad	
Glenturret	21	43			Cl	Ro		Prop	
Glenturret	5	43	–		Gr	Ro		Paisley	Tr gold label
Glenturret	8	43			Gr	Ro		Prop	old label
Glenturret	12	46			Gr	Ro		Prop	old label
Glenugie	1966	40		T	Cl	Ro	East	G&M	cc old
Glenury Royal	12	40	++		Cl	Ro	East	Prop	also G&M TP
Glenury Royal	23	53.8	++		Gr	Ro		Cad	
Glenury Royal	13	80			Gr	Ro		Cad	Tr

Malt Miniatures

Distillery	Age/Proof		Avail-ability	Shape & Colour			Area	Bottled by	Notes
Highland Park	12	40	++	T	Cl	De	Other	Prop	
Highland Park	12	40	+	T	Cl	De		Prop	10cl
Highland Park	(8)	40	++		Cl	Fl		G&M	TP Tr
Highland Park	(8)	57	++		Cl	Fl		G&M	TP Tr
Highland Park	1966	52	++		Cl	Ro		SV	
Highland Park	23	40.4	+		Gr	Ro		Cad	
Highland Park	21	46	+		Gr	Ro		Cad	
Highland Park	22	46	+		Cl	Ro		Cad	
Highland Park	(8)	70			Cl	Fl		G&M	old TP red fig
Highland Park	(8)	100			Cl	Fl		G&M	old TP red fig
Highland Park	12	70			Cl	Ro		Prop	as 10cl Tr
Highland Park	22	80			Gr	Ro		Cad	Tr
Imperial	1970	40	++	T	Cl	Ro	Spey	G&M	cc both
Imperial	1969	40	+	T	Cl	Ro		G&M	cc old
Imperial	12	65	++	T	Cl	Ro		MacA	
Inchgower	12	40	++	T	Cl	Ro	K&E	Prop	pictorial label
Inchgower	12	40	+	T	Cl	Ro		Prop	buff label
Inchgower	12	70		T	Cl	Ro		Prop	neck label
Isle of Jura	10	40	++	T	Cl	Dc	Other	Prop	boxed
Isle of Jura	8	40			Cl	Fa		Prop	
Inchmurrin		40	++	T	Cl	Ro	South	Prop	L Lomond dist
Kinclaith	1966	40	++	T	Cl	Ro	Low	G&M	cc both
Kinclaith	1967	40	+	T	Cl	Ro		G&M	cc map
Kinclaith	20	46	+		Cl	Ro		Cad	
Knockando	1976	43	++	T	Cl	Dc	Spey	Prop	boxed
Knockando	1975	43	+	T	Cl	Dc		Prop	boxed
Knockando	1974	43		T	Cl	Dc		Prop	boxed
Knockando	1973	43		T	Cl	Dc		Prop	boxed
Knockdhu	1974	40	++	T	Cl	Ro	K&E	G&M	cc both

Malt Miniatures

Distillery	Age/Proof		Avail-ability	Shape & Colour			Area	Bottled by	Notes
Lagavulin	16	43	++	T	Cl	Ro	Islay	Prop	
Lagavulin	12	43	+	T	Cl	Ro		Prop	pict label
Lagavulin	12	43		T	Cl	Ro		Prop	old label
Laphraoig	10	40	++	T	Gr	Ro	Islay	prop	in tube
Laphraoig	1967	40		T	Cl	Ro		G&M	cc old
Laphraoig	10	40			Gr	Fa		Prop	also 43
Laphraoig	10	70		T	Gr	Ro		Prop	also 75, Cl, Tr
Linkwood	12	40	++	T	Cl	Ro	K&E	Prop	
Linkwood	15	40	++	T	Cl	Ro		G&M	
Linkwood	15	40	++		Cl	Fl		G&M	TP
Linkwood	15	57	++		Cl	Fl		G&M	TP
Linkwood	25	40	++		Cl	Fl		G&M	TP
Linkwood	26	40	++	T	Cl	Ro		G&M	RW (A&S)
Linkwood	12	70			Cl	Fa		Prop	white label
Linkwood	(12)	70			Cl	Fl		G&M	TP Tr
Linkwood	(12)	100			Cl	Fl		G&M	TP
Linkwood	12				Gr	Ro		Prop	Tr Black label
Linkwood	5	40			Cl	Fl		Prop	white label
Littlemill	8	(40)		T	Cl	Ro	Low	Prop	
Littlemill	5	(40)		T	Cl	Ro		Prop	also Fa, Gr
Lochnagar	12	40	+	T	Cl	Ro	East	Prop	2 labels
Lochnagar	1969	40		T	Cl	Ro		G&M	cc old
Lochnagar	1970	40		T	Cl	Ro		G&M	cc old
Lochside	1966	43	++		Cl	Ro	East	SV	
Lochside	1965	40		T	Cl	Ro		G&M	cc old
Longmorn	15	43	++	T	Cl	Ro	K&E	Prop	in tube
Longmorn	12	40	++	T	Cl	Ro		G&M	
Longmorn	12	40	++		Cl	Fl		G&M	TP Tr
Longmorn	1974	46	+		Cl	Ro		SV	
Longmorn	12	57	++		Cl	Fl		G&M	TP
Longmorn	13	46	++		Gr	Ro		Cad	
Longmorn	21	46	+		Cl	Ro		Cad	

Malt Miniatures

Distillery	Age/Proof		Avail-ability	Shape & Colour			Area	Bottled by	Notes
Macallan	10	40	++	T	Cl	Ro	Spey	Prop	
Macallan	1972	43	++	T	Cl	Ro		Prop	
Macallan	1971	43	++	T	Cl	Ro		Prop	
Macallan	1970	43	+	T	Cl	Ro		Prop	
Macallan	1969	43	+	T	Cl	Ro		Pro	
Macallan	18	54.9	++		Gr	Ro		Cad	
Macallan	1949	37.9	+		Cl	Ro		SV	limited edition
Macallan	1968	43		T	Cl	Ro		Prop	
Macallan	1967	43		T	Cl	Ro		Prop	
Macallan	1966	43		T	Cl	Ro		Prop	
Macallan	1965	43		T	Cl	Ro		Prop	
Macallan	1964	43		T	Cl	Ro		Prop	
Macallan	1963	43		T	Cl	Ro		Prop	
Macallan	7	43		T	Cl	Ro		Prop	Italy
Macallan	8	43		T	Cl	Ro		Prop	France
Macallan	12	80			Cl	Ro		Prop	boxed
Macallan	12	75			Cl	Ro		Prop	
Macallan	16	43			Cl	Ro		Prop	
Macallan					Gr	Ro			trade bottling
Macallan		70			Cl	Fl		G&M	
Macallan		100			Cl	Fl		G&M	
Macallan	1937	70			Cl	Fl		G&M	MBC88
Macallan	15	70			Cl	Fl		G&M	TP
Macallan	15	100			Cl	Fl		G&M	TP
Macallan	12	70			Cl	Fl		G&M	TP
Macallan	12	100			Cl	Fl		G&M	TP
Macallan	10	70			Cl	Fl		G&M	TP
Macallan	10	100			Cl	Fl		G&M	TP
Macallan	18	80			Gr	Ro		Cad	
Macallan		103		T	Cl	Ro			'As We Get It'
Macduff	1975	40	++	T	Cl	Ro	K&E	G&M	cc both
Millburn	1971	40	++	T	Cl	Ro	North	G&M	cc map
Millburn	1966	40	+	T	Cl	Ro		G&M	cc both
Miltonduff	1963	40	++	T	Cl	Ro	K&E	G&M	cc both
Miltonduff	1964	40	+	T	Cl	Ro		G&M	cc map
(Mosstowie)	1970	40	++	T	Cl	Ro		G&M	cc both
(Mosstowie)	1975	40	+	T	Cl	Ro		G&M	cc map
Mortlach	15	40	++	T	Cl	Ro	Spey	G&M	
Mortlach	12	40	++		Cl	Fl		G&M	TP
Mortlach	12	57	++		Cl	Fl		G&M	TP
Mortlach	26	40	++	T	Cl	Ro		G&M	R Wed (A&S)
Mortlach	50	40	++		Cl	Ro		G&M	
Mortlach	12	43			Cl	Fa			Japan MBC88
Mortlach	22	80			Gr	Ro		Cad	Tr

Malt Miniatures

Distillery	Age/Proof		Avail-ability	Shape & Colour			Area	Bottled by	Notes
North Port	1970	40	++	T	Cl	Ro	East	G&M	cc both
Oban	14	43	++	T	Cl	Ro	South	Prop	
Oban	12	40	+	T	Cl	Dc		Prop	Tr also Fa
Old Pulteney	8	40	++		Cl	Fl	North	G&M	TP
Old Pulteney	8	57	++		Cl	Fl		G&M	TP
Old Pulteney	8	40			Cl	Fl		G&M	TP plain label
Old Pulteney	8	57			Cl	Fl		G&M	TP plain label
Ord	12	40	++	T	Cl	Ro	North	Prop	Glenordie
Ord	27	55.4	++		Gr	Ro		Cad	
Pittyvaich	12	54	++		Cl	Ro	Spey	MacA	
Pittyvaich	11	56.6	++		Gr	Ro		Cad	2 labels
Port Ellen	1971	40	++	T	Cl	Ro	Islay	G&M	cc both
Port Ellen	1970	40	+	T	Cl	Ro		G&M	cc map
Port Ellen	1974	40	+	T	Cl	Ro		G&M	cc map
Port Ellen	1969	40	+	T	Cl	Ro		G&M	cc old
Port Ellen	12	62.7	++	T	Cl	Ro		MacA	
Rosebank	8	40	++	T	Gr	Ro	Low	Prop	
Rosebank	17	46			Cl	Ro		Cad	
Rosebank	12	43			Gr	Ro		Prop	Japan
Royal Brackla	1970	40	++	T	Cl	Ro	K&E	G&M	cc both
Royal Brackla	1972	40	+	T	Cl	Ro		G&M	cc map
Royal Brackla	1969	40	+	T	Cl	Ro		G&M	cc old
Royal Brackla	12	45	++	T	Cl	Ro		MacA	

Malt Miniatures

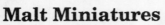

Distillery	Age/Proof		Avail-ability	Shape & Colour		Area	Bottled by	Notes
St Magdalene	15	80		Gr	Ro	Low	Cad	Tr
Scapa	8	40	++	Cl	Fl	Other	G&M	TP Longship
Scapa	8	57	++	Cl	Fl		G&M	TP Longship
Scapa	24	45.6	++	Gr	Ro		Cad	also at 50.1%
Scapa	8	40		Cl	Fl		G&M	TP plain Tr
Scapa	8	57		Cl	Fl		G&M	TP plain
Speyburn	1971	40	++ T	Cl	Ro	Spey	G&M	cc both
Springbank	5	46	+	Cl	Ro	Camp	Prop	Tr
Springbank	8	46	+	Cl	Ro		Prop	Tr
Springbank	10	46	+	Cl	Ro		Prop	
Springbank	12	46	++ T	Cl	Ro		Prop	
Springbank	15	46	++	Cl	Ro		Prop	
Springbank	21	46	++	Cl	Ro		Prop	
Springbank	1967	46	++	Cl	Ro		SV	also Prestonfield
Springbank	12	59.8	++	Cl	Ro		MacA	
(Longrow)	1973	46	++ T	Cl	Ro		Prop	pict label
(Longrow)	14	46	++	Cl	Ro		Prop	
(Longrow)	1973	43		Cl	Ro		Prop	plain label, 46
Springbank	1952	45.5		Cl	Ro		Prop	limited nos
Springbank	5	80		Cl	Fa		Prop	Tr
Springbank	5	80		Gr	Ro		Prop	Italy
Springbank	8	80		Gr	Ro		Prop	Tr
Springbank	17	80		Gr	Ro		Prop	Cad label Tr
Springbank	21	46		Cl	Ro		Prop	Cad label
Springbank	1919		T	Gr	Ro		Prop	very limited nos
Strathisla	8	40	++ T	Cl	Ro	K&E	G&M	
Strathisla	8	40	++	Cl	Fl		G&M	TP
Strathisla	8	57	++	Cl	Fl		G&M	TP
Strathisla	10	70		Cl	Ro		Prop	Tr
Strathisla	20	40		Cl	Fl		G&M	TP RW (C&D)
Strathisla	8	70		Cl	Fl		G&M	TP old label
Strathisla	8	100		Cl	Fl		G&M	TP old label
Strathisla		70		Cl	Fl		G&M	Milton Distillery
Strathisla				Cl	De		Prop	pear shape

Malt Miniatures

Distillery	Age	Proof	Avail-ability	Shape		Colour	Area	Bottled by	Notes
Talisker	10	45.8	++	T	Cl	Ro	Other	Prop	
Talisker	8	45.8	++	T	Cl	Ro		Prop	
Talisker	(8)	70			Cl	Fl		G&M	TP Tr
Talisker	(8)	100			Cl	Fl		G&M	TP
Talisker	8	70			Cl	Fl		G&M	TP old label Tr
Tamdhu	10	40	++	T	Cl	Ro	Spey	Prop	'cut out' label
Tamdhu	10	40	++	T	Cl	Ro		Prop	pictorial label Tr
Tamdhu	8	40	++		Cl	Fl		G&M	TP
Tamdhu	8	70		T	Cl	Ro		Prop	brown label
Tamnavulin	10	40	++	T	Cl	Ro	Spey	Prop	
Tamnavulin	20	46	+		Cl	Ro		Cad	
Tamnavulin	(8)	40			Cl	Ro		Prop	Tr also Rd
Tamnavulin		75			Gr	Ro		Prop	Tr also Cl Fa
Tobermory		40			Gr	Ro	Other	Prop	see page 49
Tobermory	8	43			Gr	Ro		Prop	export
Tobermory	10	43			Gr	Ro		Prop	export
Tobermory	12	43			Gr	Ro		Prop	export
(Ledaig)	1973	40	+	T	Cl	Ro		G&M	cc both
(Ledaig)	1972	40	+	T	Cl	Ro		G&M	cc both
Tomatin	10	43	++	T	Cl	Ro	North	Prop	new label
Tomatin	10	43	++	T	Cl	Ro		Prop	PET
Tomatin	1968	40	++	T	Cl	Ro		G&M	cc map
Tomatin	1966	46	++	T	Cl	Ro		SV	
Tomatin	1970	40	+	T	Cl	Ro		G&M	cc both
Tomatin	13	60.5	++		Gr	Ro		Cad	
Tomatin	5	43			Cl	Ro		Prop	Holland
Tomintoul	(8)	43	++		Cl	Fa	Spey	Prop	new label
Tomintoul	12							Prop	
Tomintoul	1971	40	++		Cl	Ro		SV	
Tomintoul	(8)	40			Cl	Rd		Prop	also Fa & PET
Tormore	10	43	++	T	Cl	Ro	Spey	Prop	light label
Tormore	10	43	+	T	Cl	De		Prop	red label also Ro
Tormore	10	43			Cl	Fa		Prop	old label
Tullibardine	10	40	++		Cl	Ro		Prop	Tr
Tullibardine		70			Gr	Ro			Tr plain label
Tullibardine	12	80			Cl	Fl			corked

Notes

The newsletters of the Mini Bottle Club have included detailed profiles of the miniatures issued over the years containing the following malt whiskies:

Aberlour–September '87; Bowmore–September '88; Auchentoshan–May '88; Bells Malts–November '86; Cadenhead issues–March '89; Cardhu–May '89; Connoisseur's Choice–January, March, May, July '89 and March '90; Glendronach–November '89; Glenfarclas–March '87, July, September '89; Glen Grant–September, November '87; Highland Park–March, May '89; Islay malts–January '86; Macallan–January, May, September '86 and November '88

The product of most of the Scottish distilleries have been bottled either by the proprietors or by merchants. In some cases the bottling has been limited to the 75cl size while in other cases stocks have been restricted to overseas markets. There follows a list of those malt distilleries that have not been represented significantly among miniature bottlings:

Allt A' Bhainne	Built 1975. Stocks are controlled by Chivas Brothers
Aultmore	*See page 56*
Ardmore	*See page 55*
Ben Wyvis	Disused pot stills at Invergordon distillery
Braes of Glenlivet	Producing since 1974. Stocks controlled by Chivas Brothers
Brora	The original Clynelish distillery, now dismantled
Glenglassaugh	*See page 54*
Glentauchers	Limited issue in France only
Glen Spey	Operated by IDV
Kininvie	New distillery in 1990
Ladyburn	Pot stills at Girvan distillery. Has been bottled in a very limited edition by Cadenhead. *See page 58*
Inverleven	Three pot stills (one 'lomond') within the Dumbarton distillery complex
Mannochmore	Distillery built in 1971 by SMD, alongside Glenlossie
Strathmill	Owned, like Glen Spey, by IDV
Teaninich	Bottled only in limited numbers by Cadenhead. *See page 58*

The Rale Last Drappie
and
Wee Deoch an Dorus
O' Pre War
Scots Usquaebaugh
Mauted Brewed
Stilled and Preed
August 1914

by J Dewar
Perth

from the label on a miniature decanter,
sealed with a tartan ribbon and contained
along with a pack of cards in a leather 'book'
entiled 'Golden Treasury'